Illustrious
Too

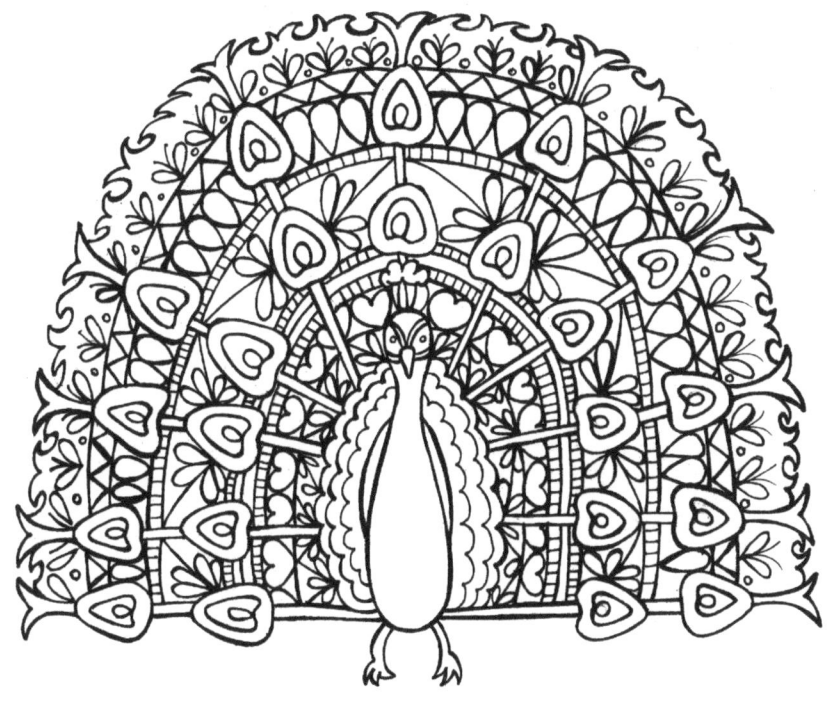

By

Akeem Wayne

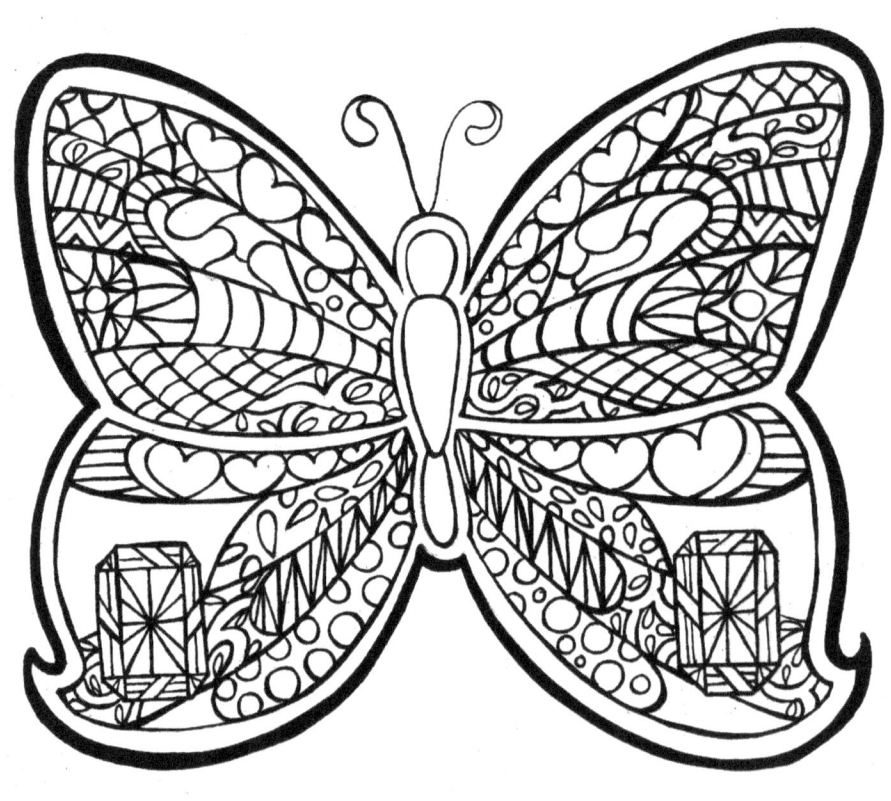

Illustrious was inspired by the birth of humanity. I created Illustrious with the ideas and theories that motivate me to create all my artwork. I create my coloring books (and all my artwork) to pay homage to a woman most scientists and archaeologists call the "Mother of Humanity". I'm truly inspired and motivated to create by the scientific facts that state that life originated on land we now call Africa, and that the first "race" is what we would call "black", and that through evolution we now have the diverse world we live in today. The work I create is my ode to our Mother.

~ Akeem Wayne

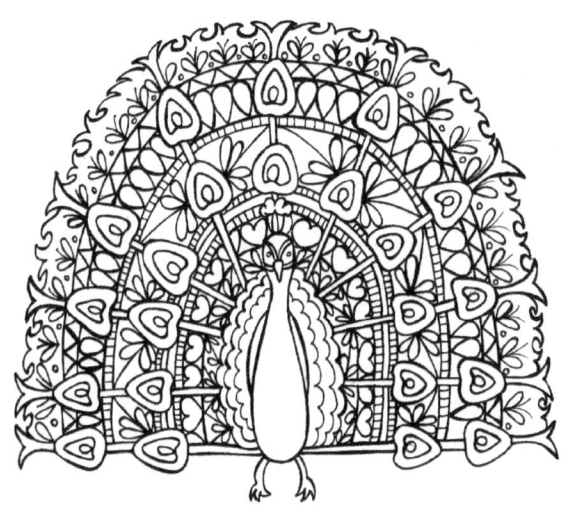

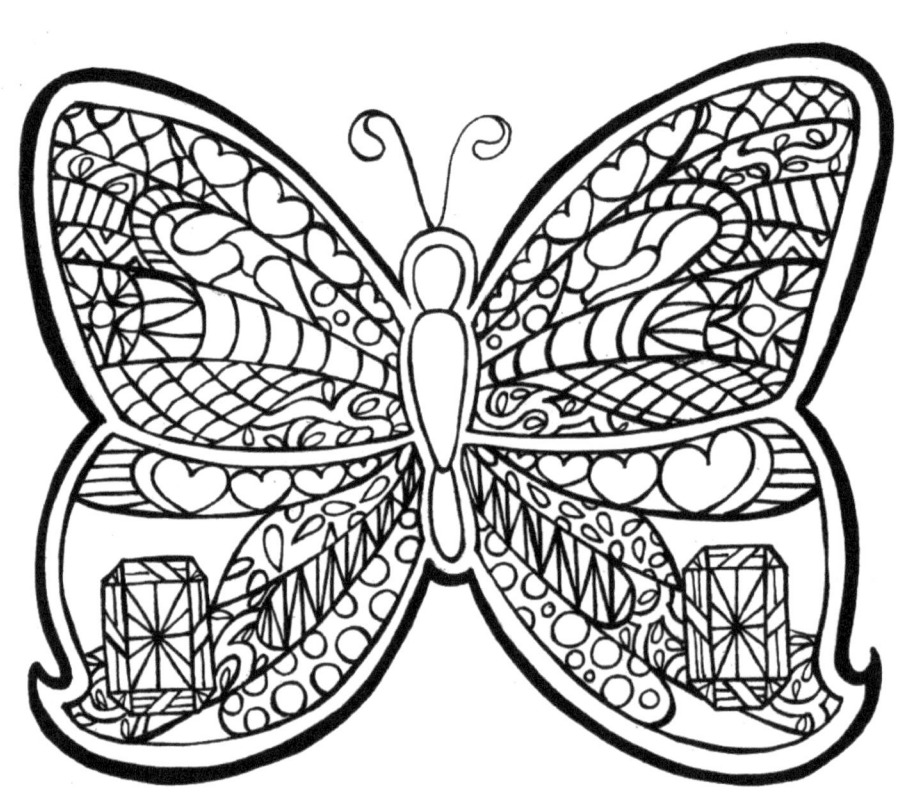

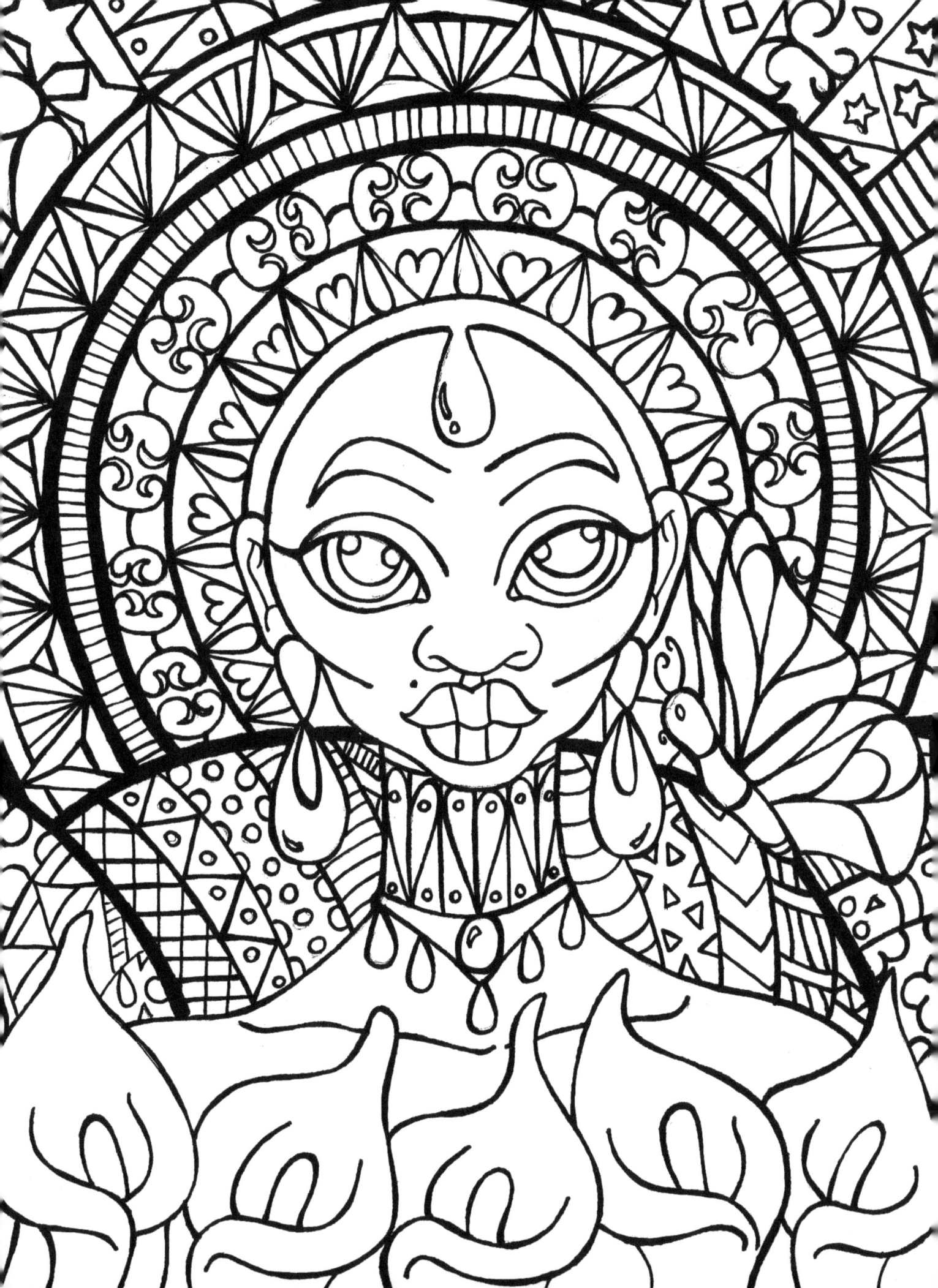

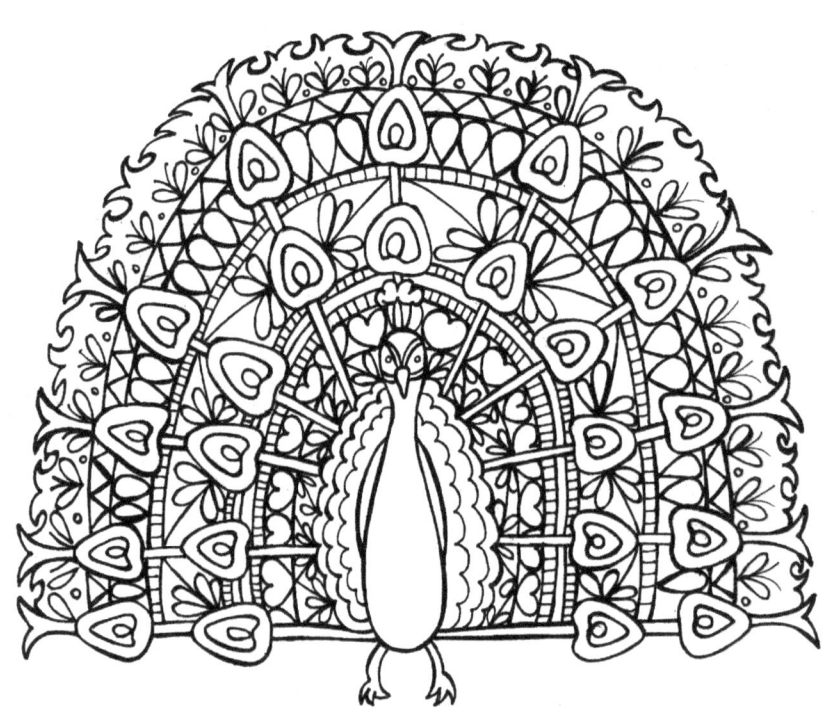

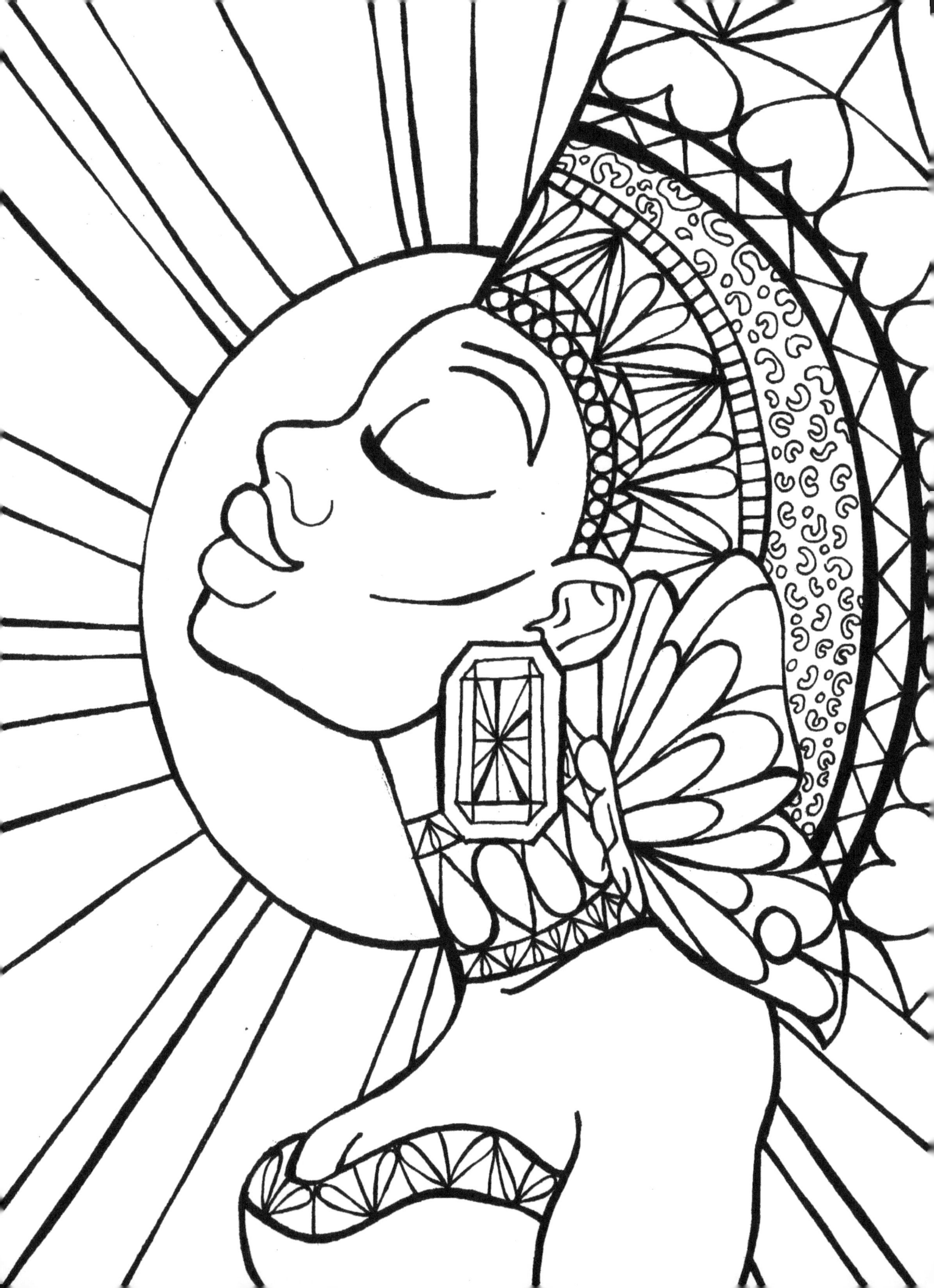

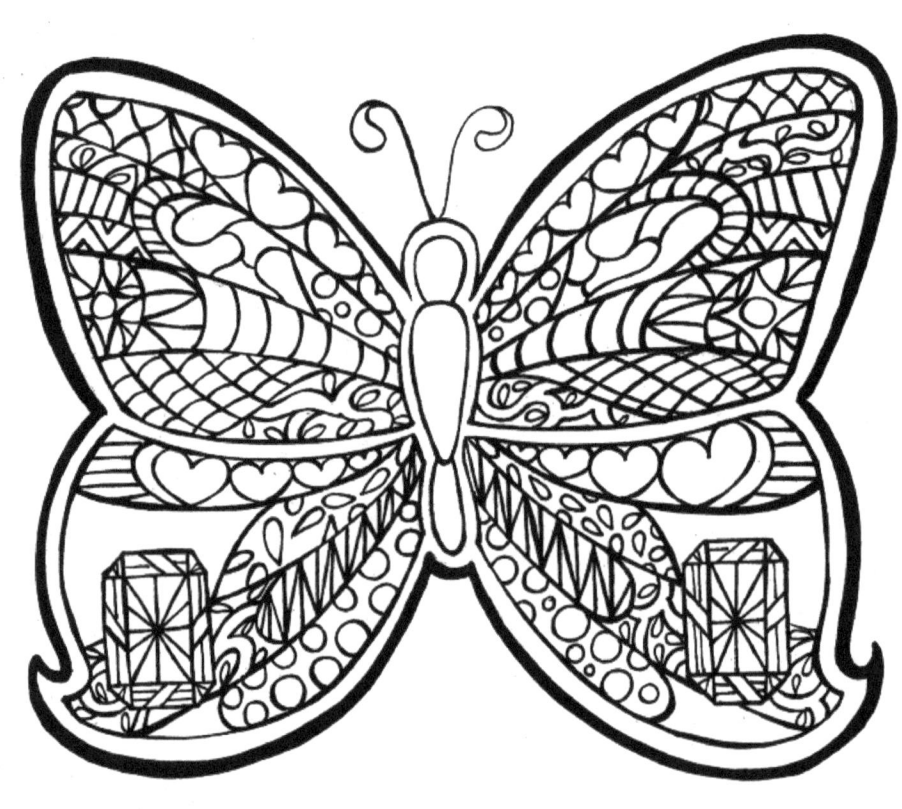

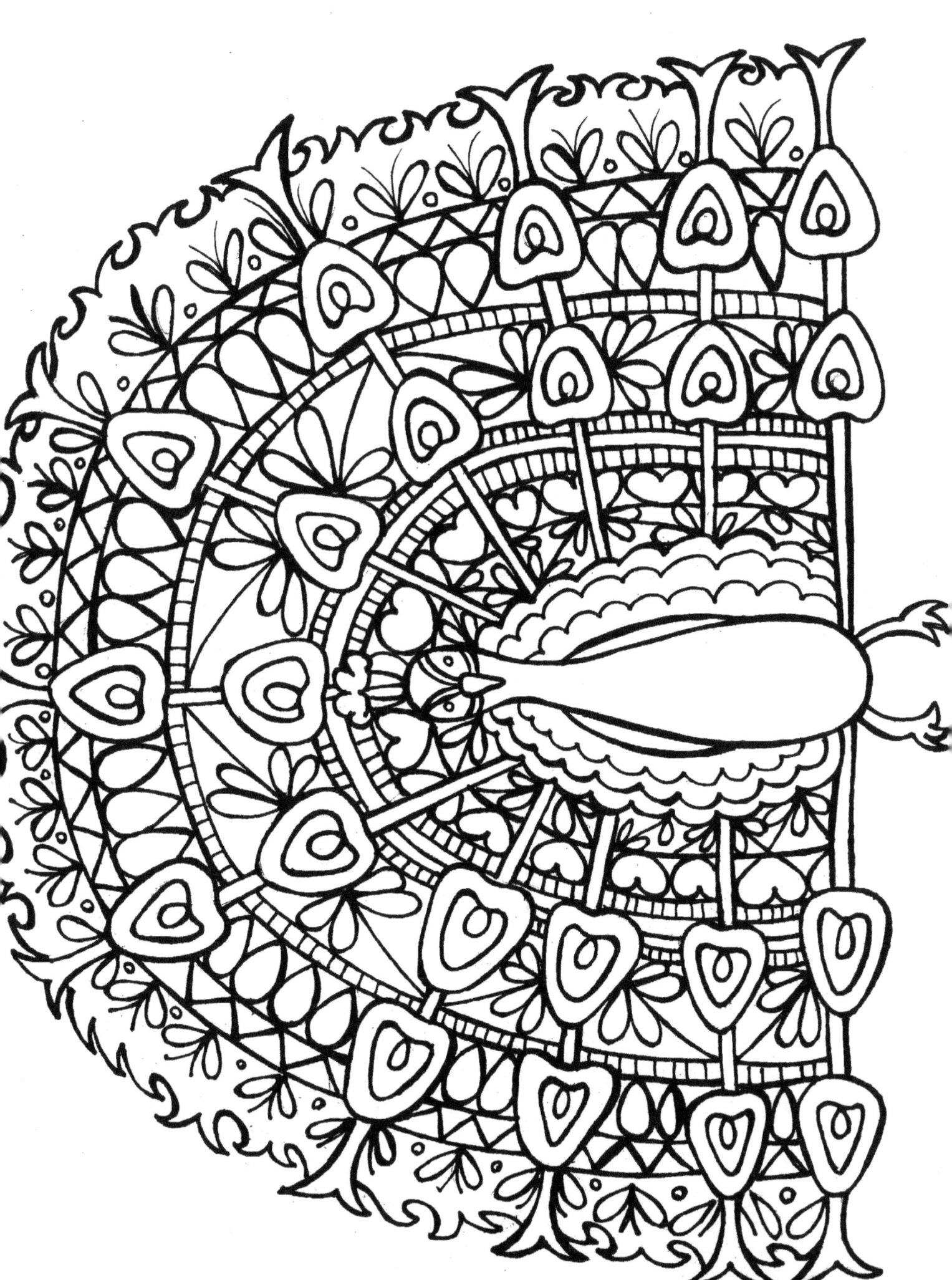

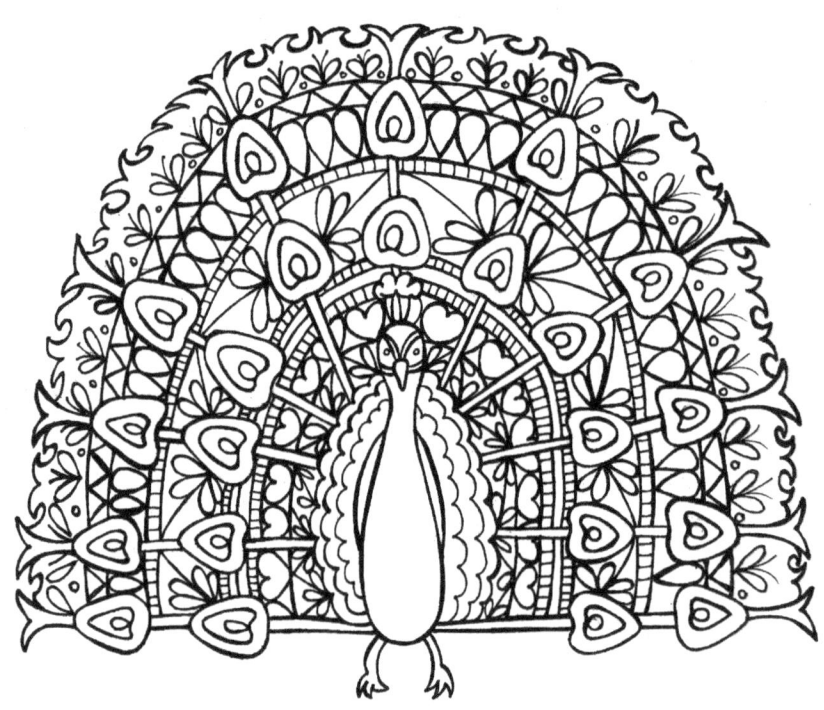

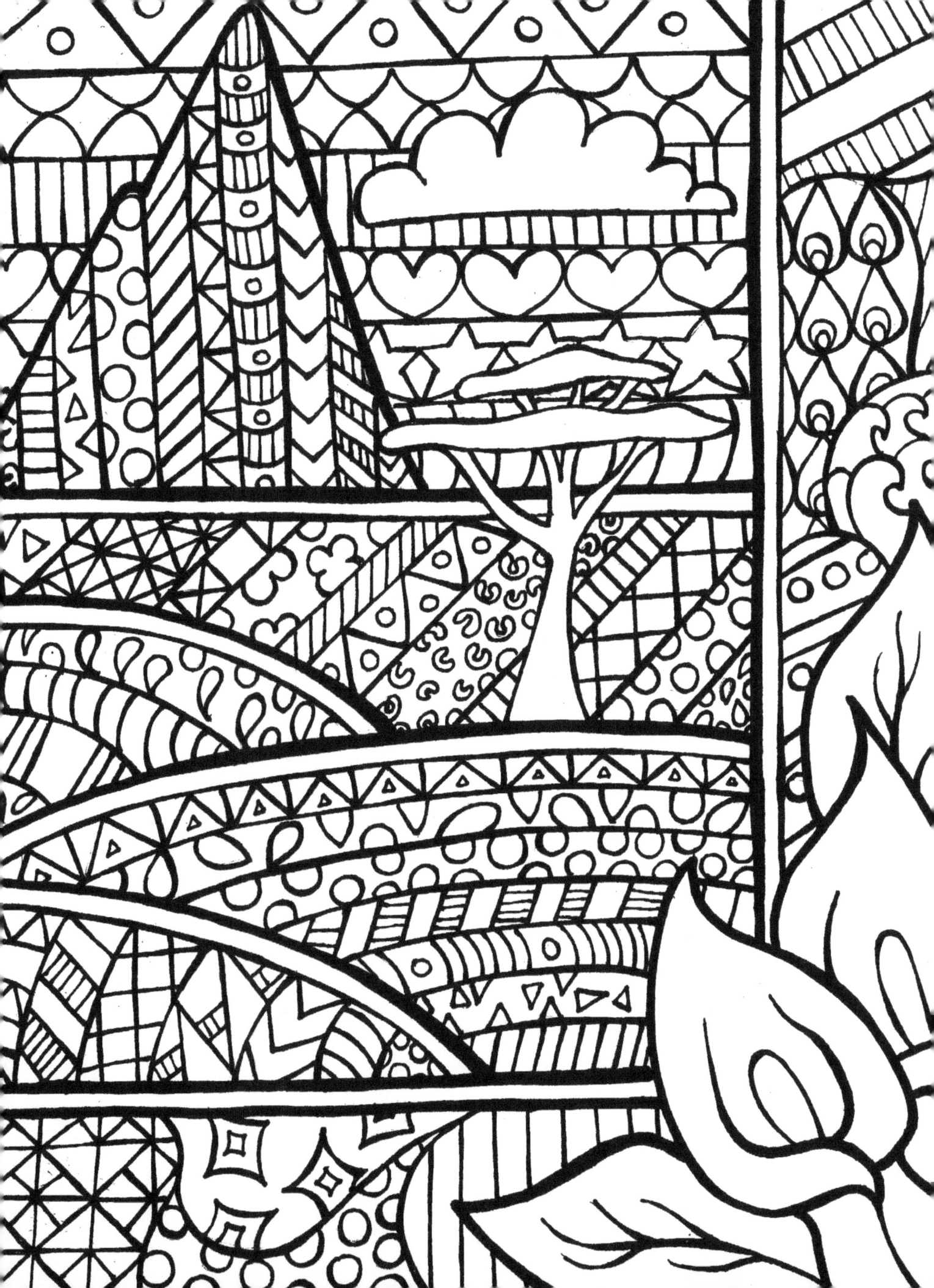

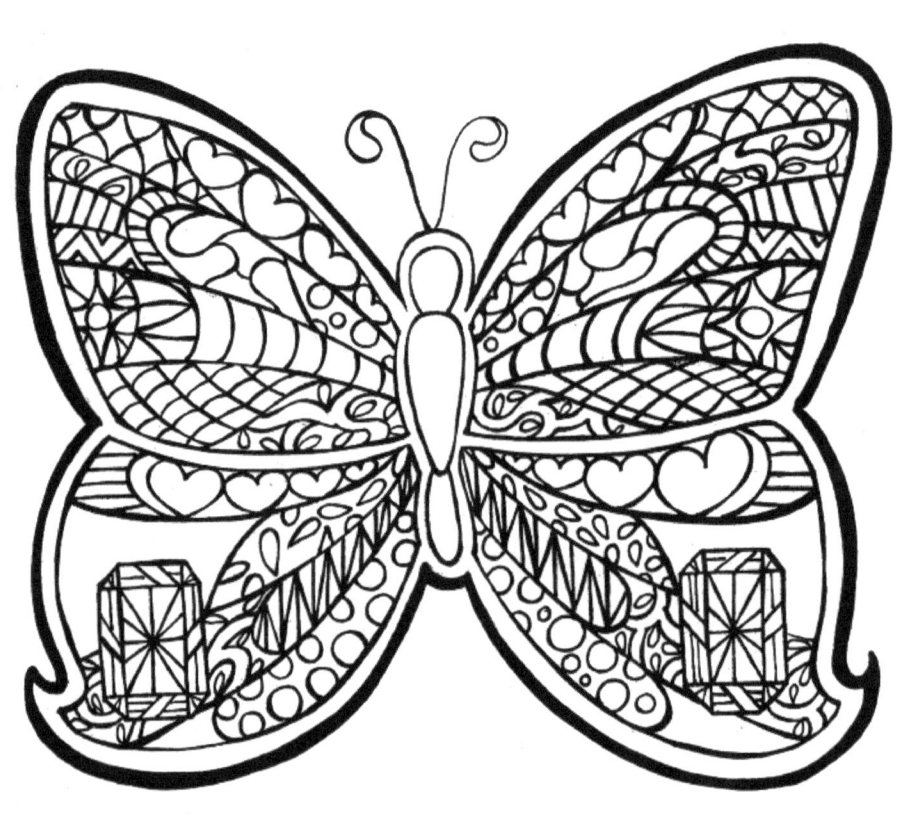

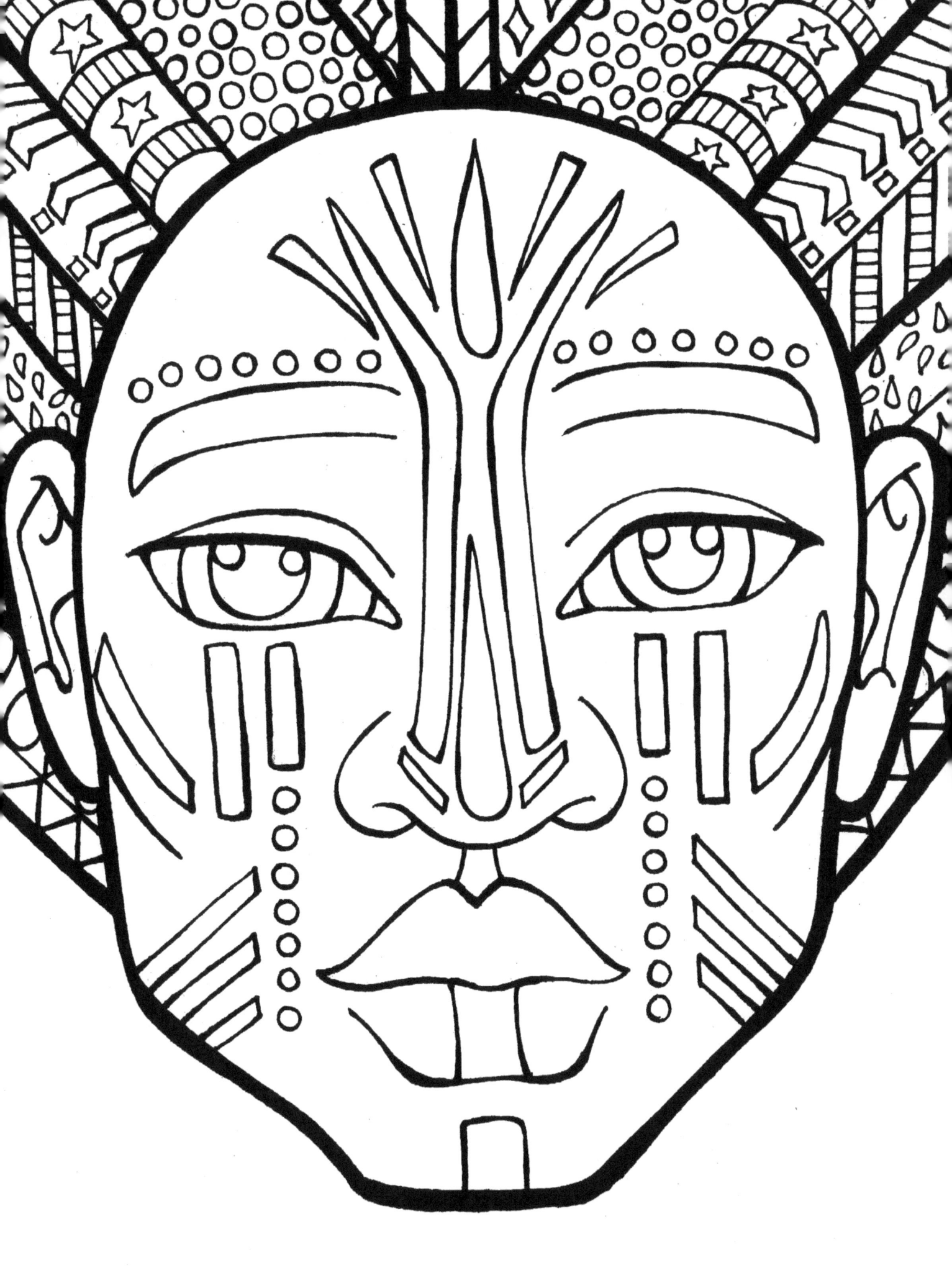

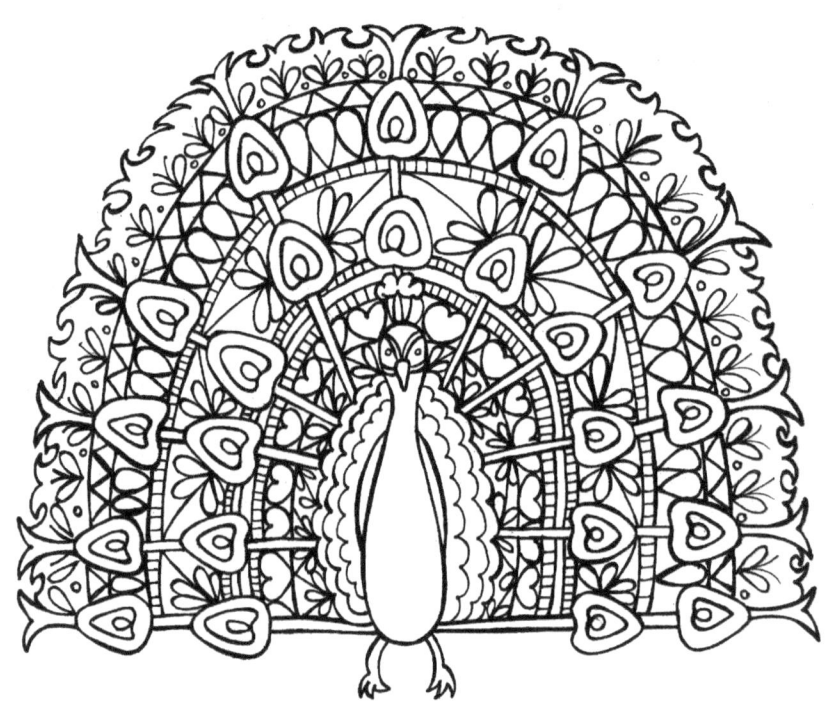

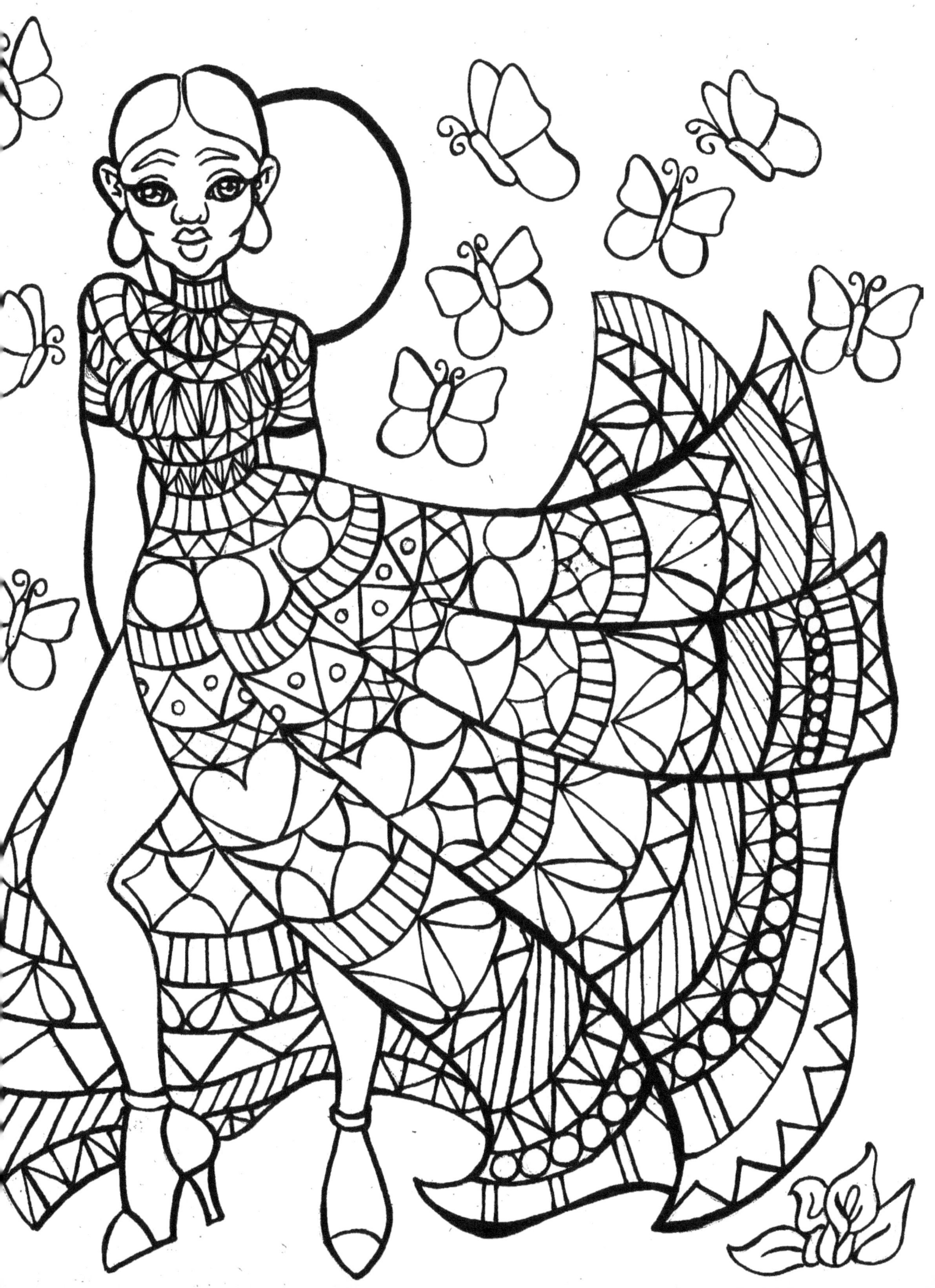

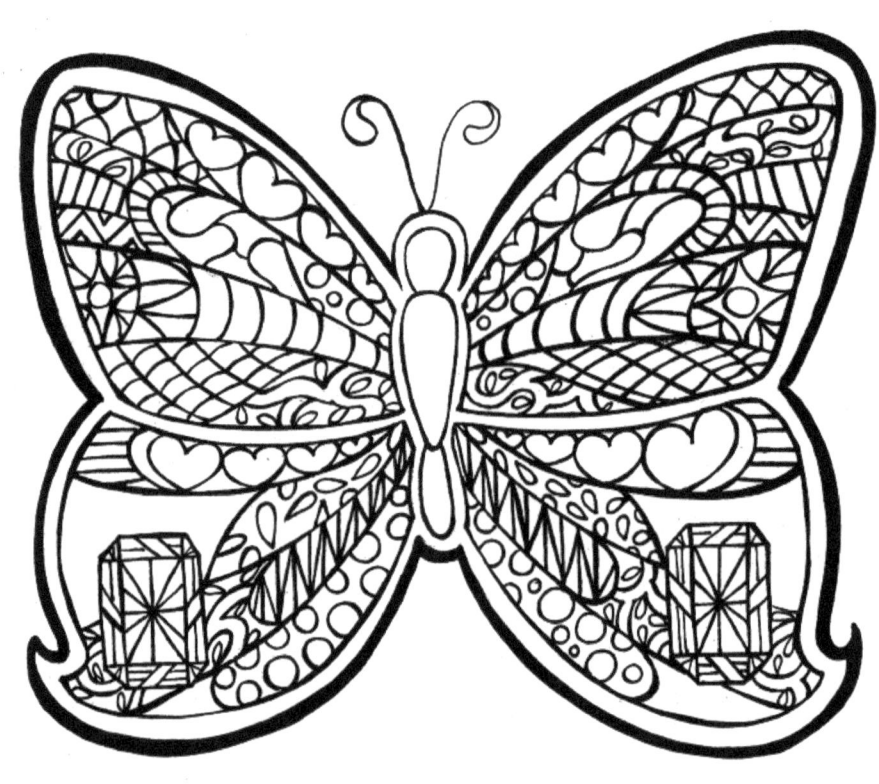

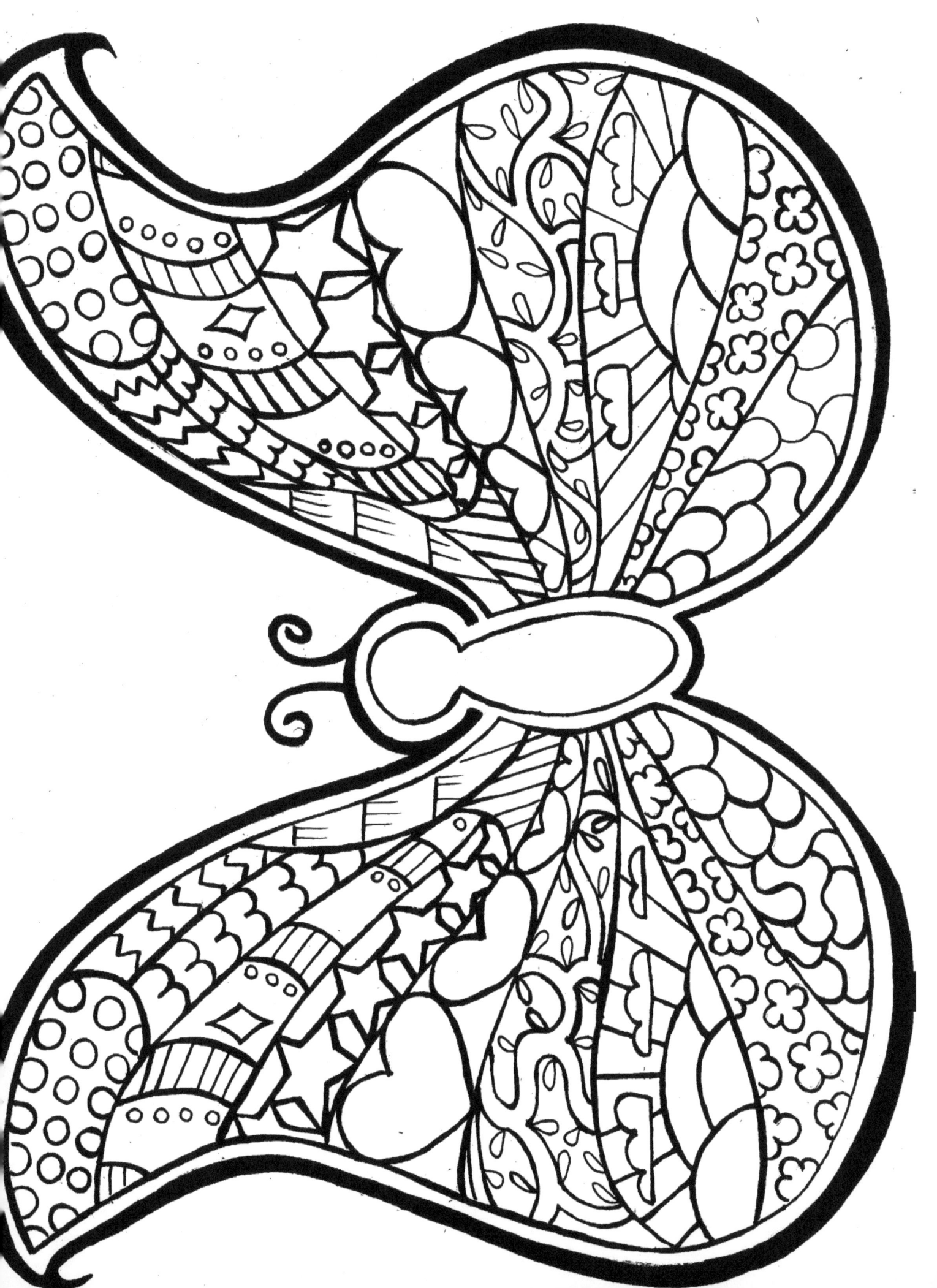

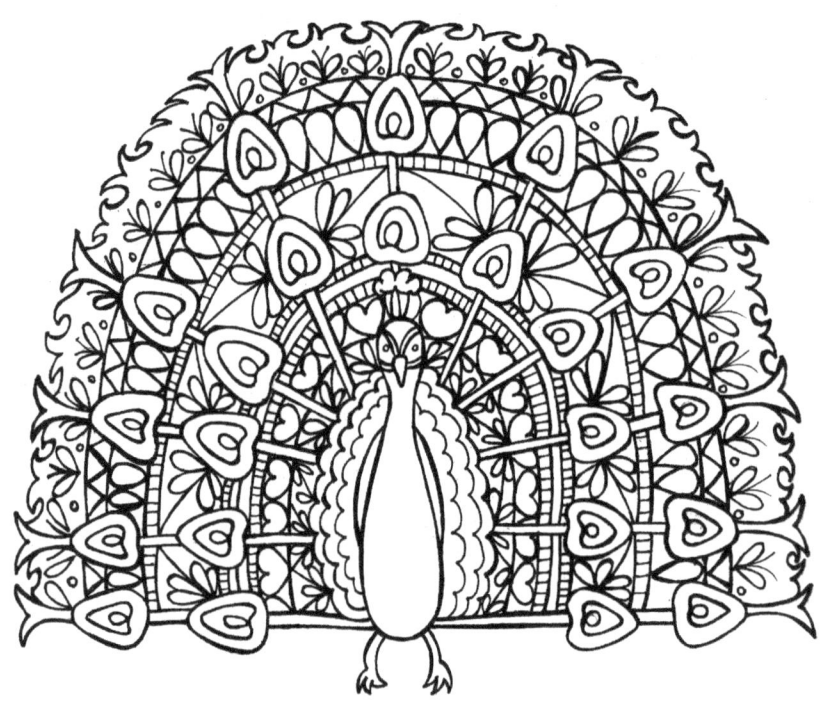

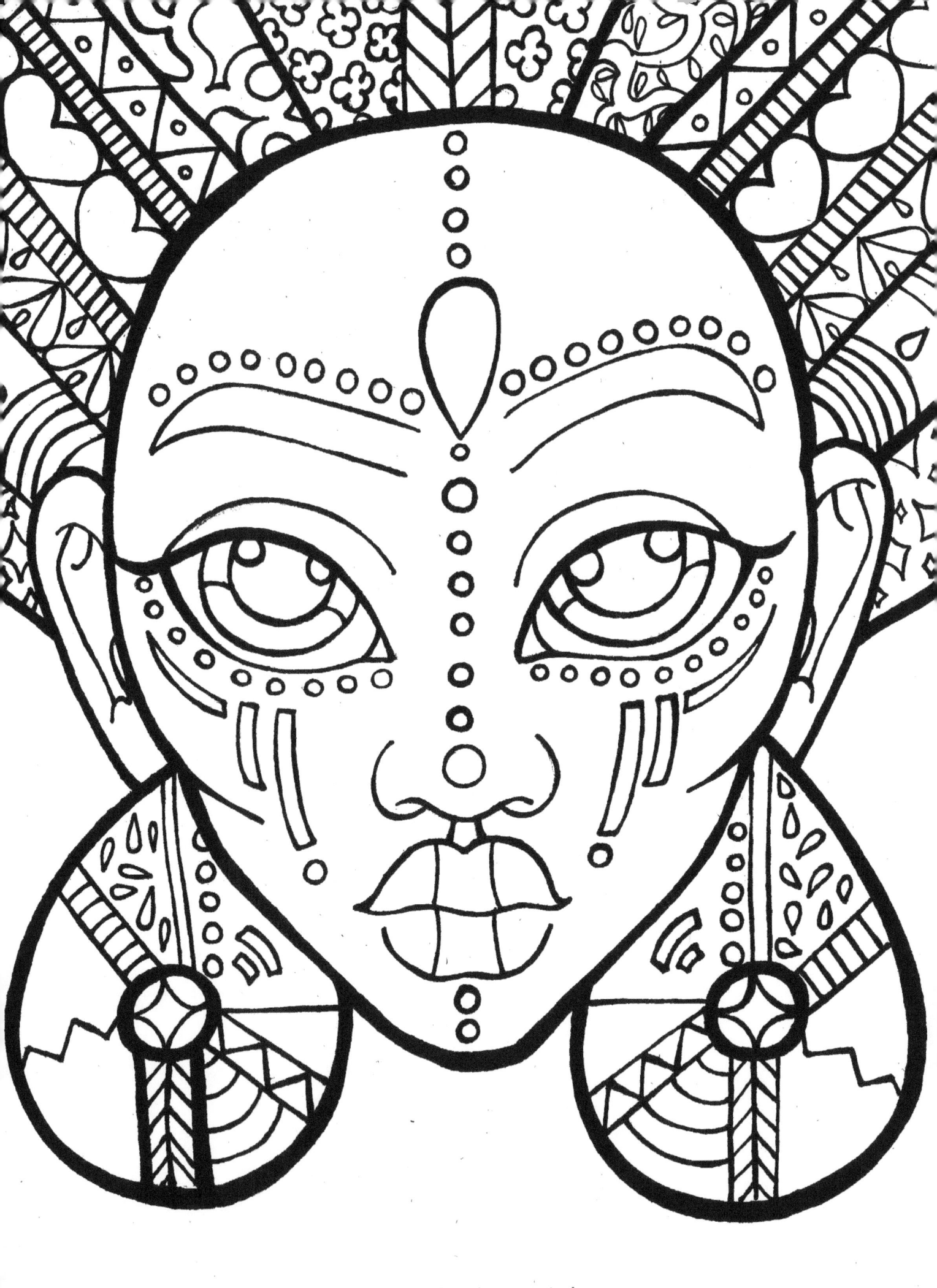

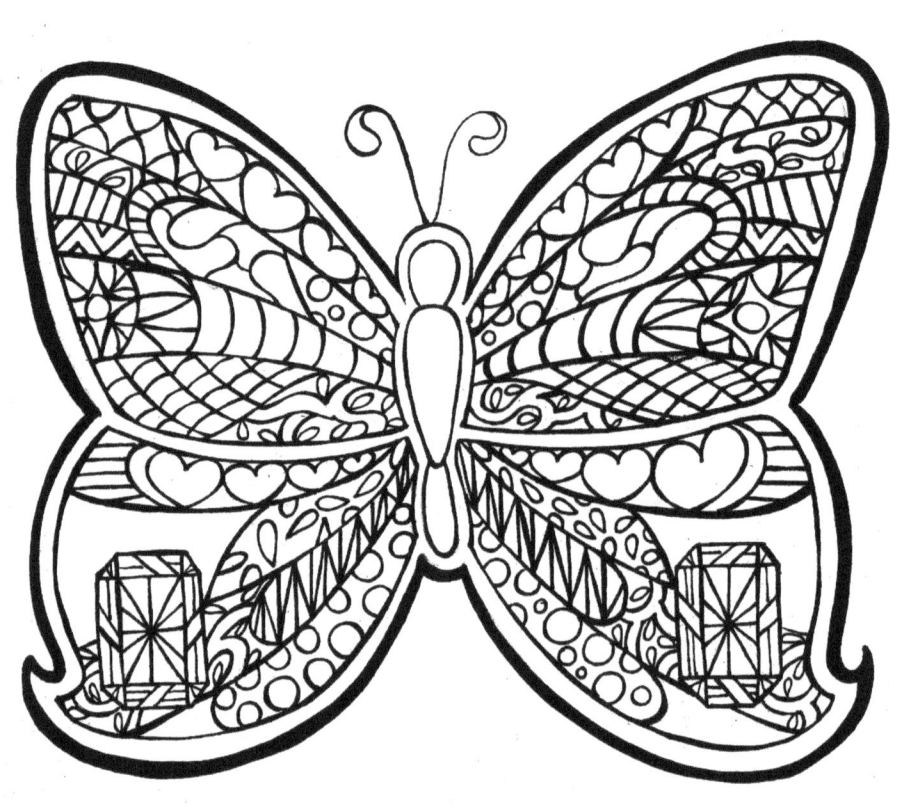

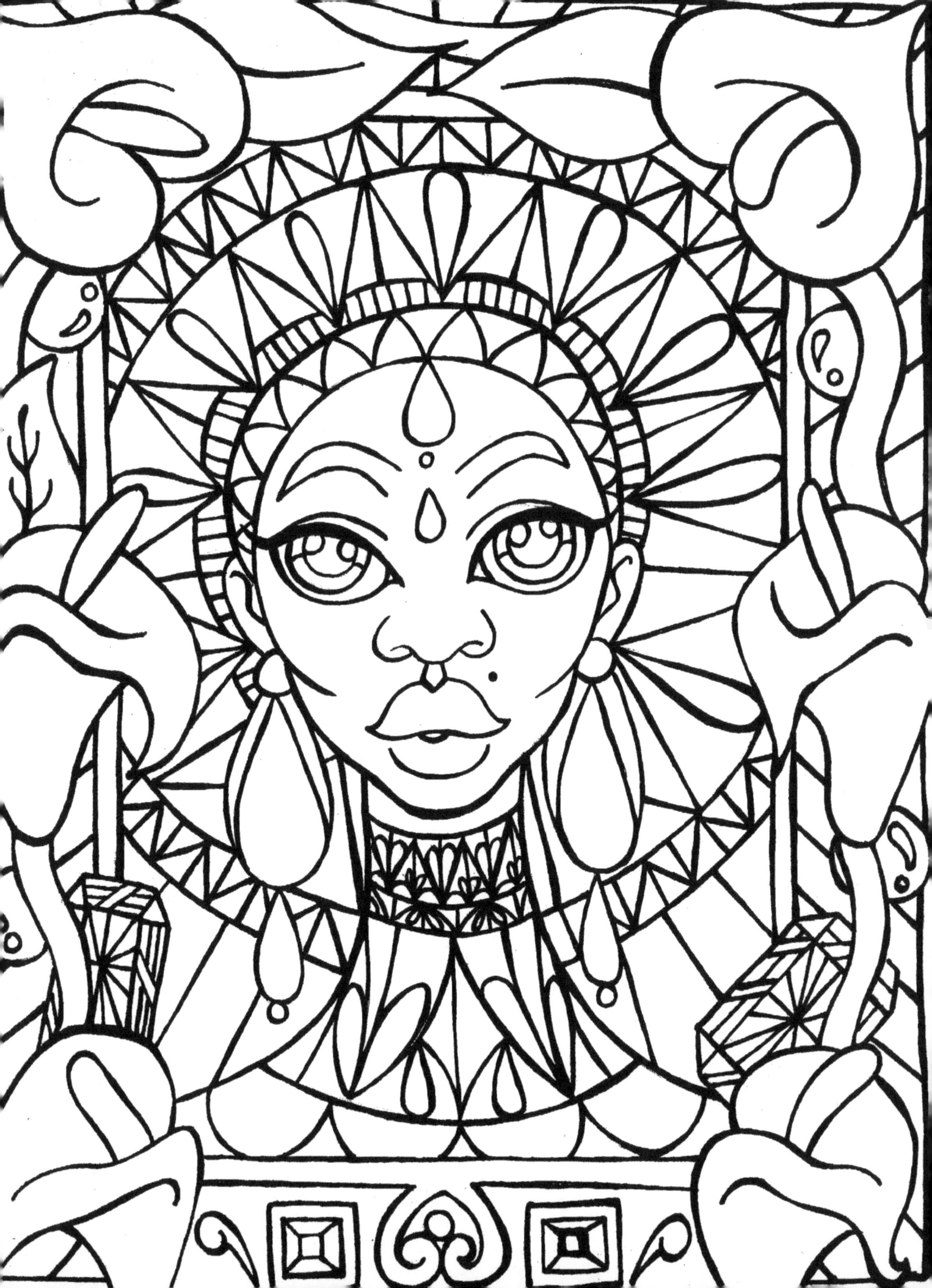

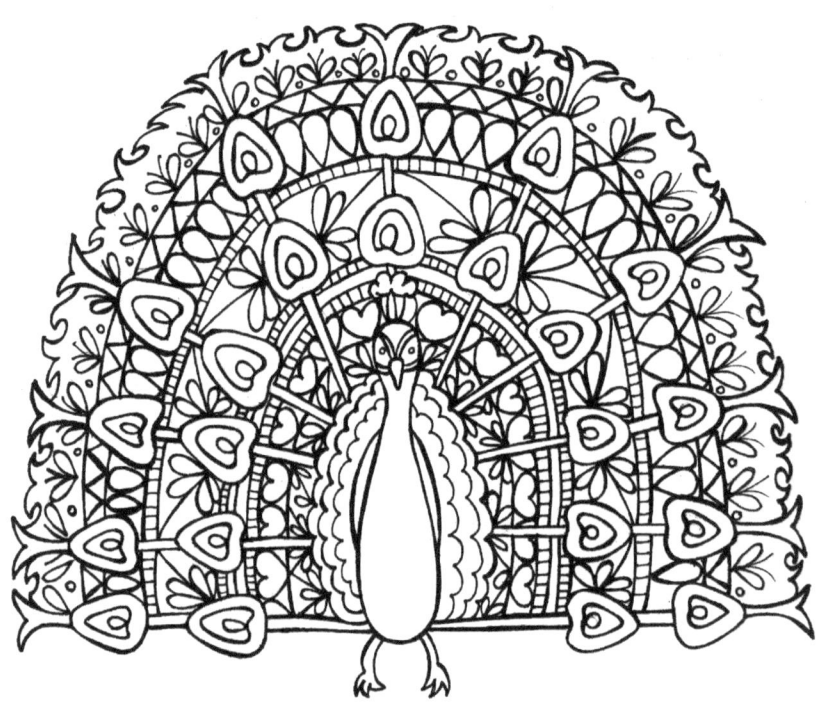

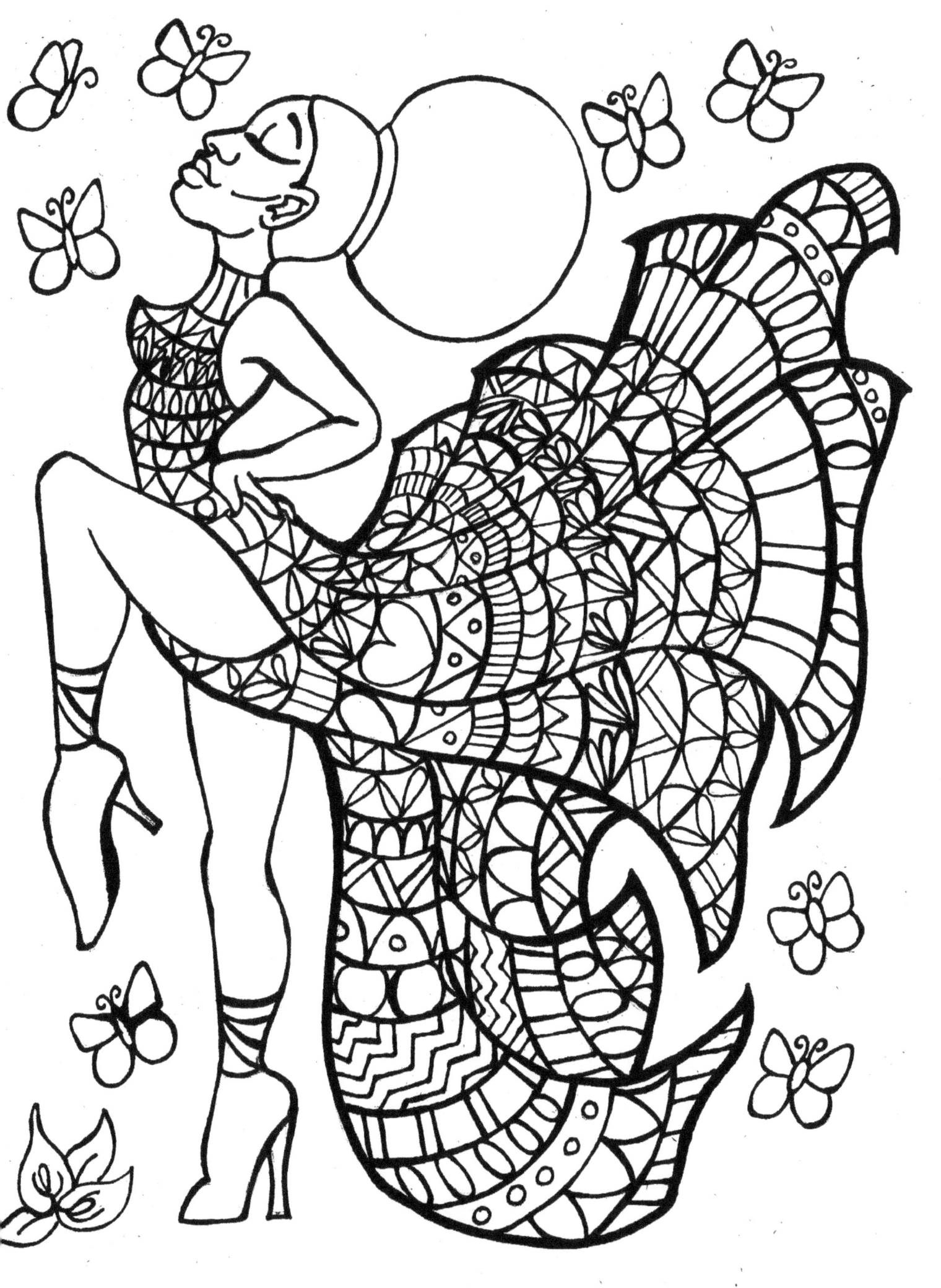

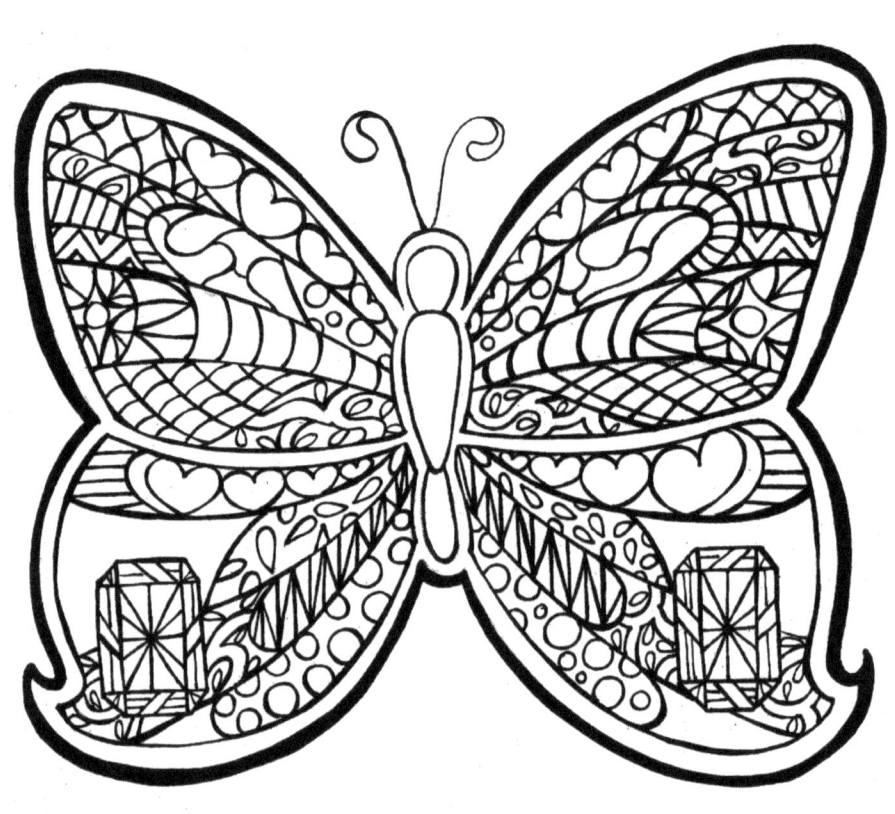

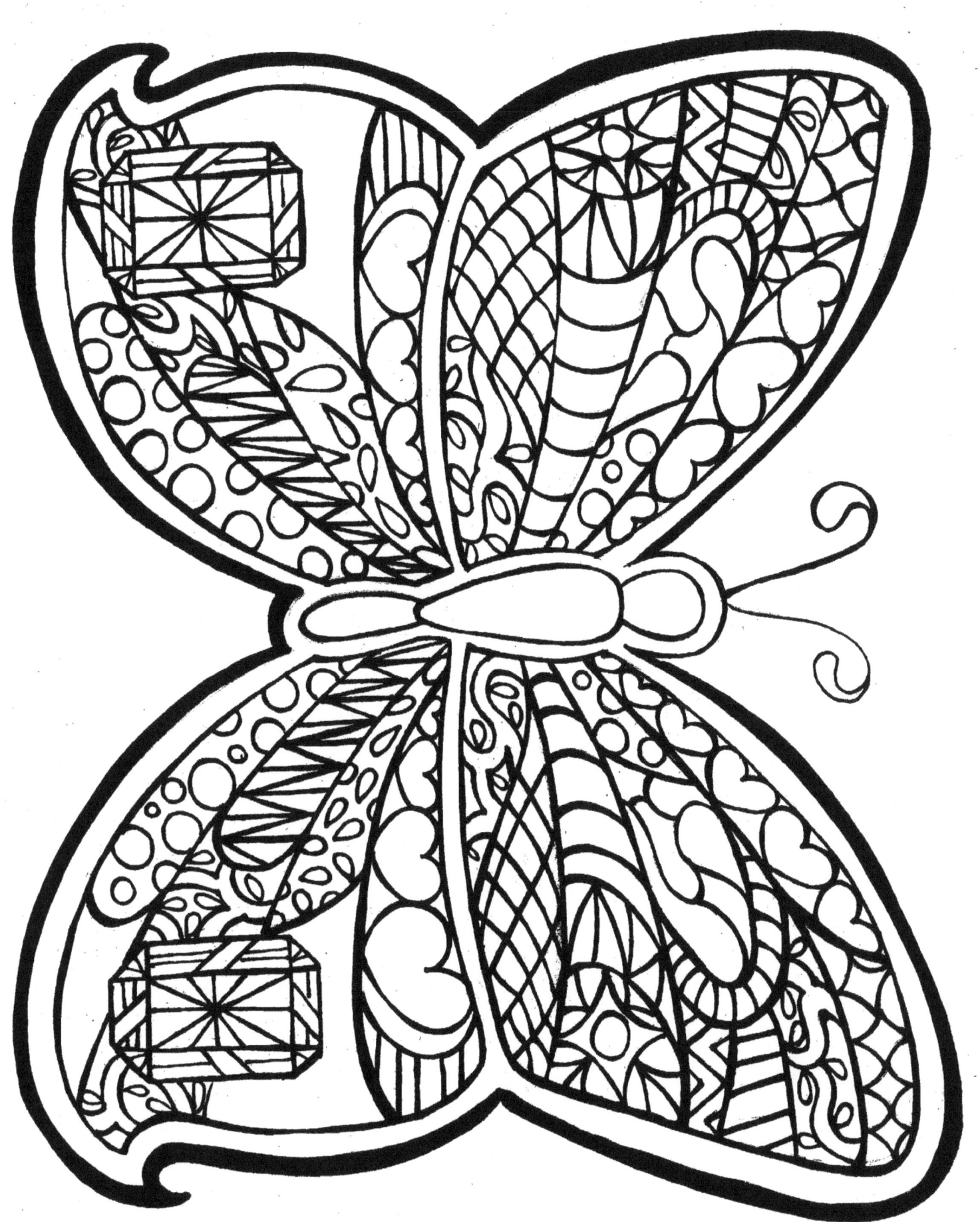

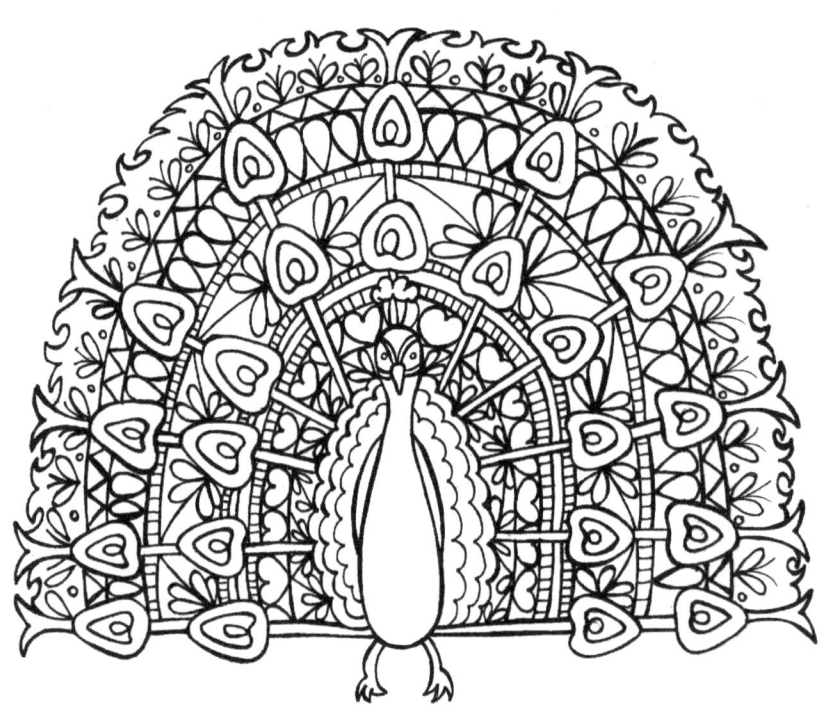

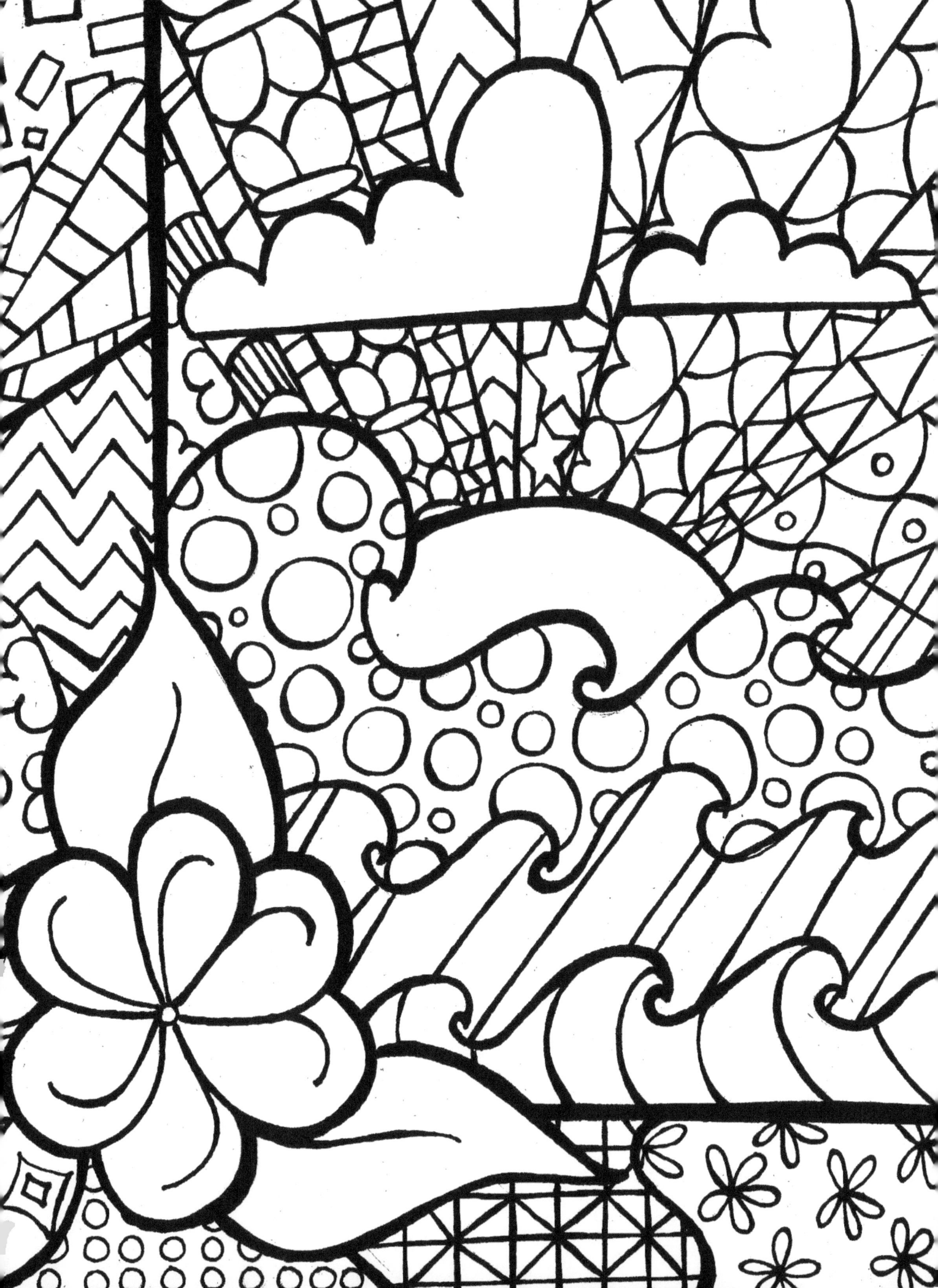

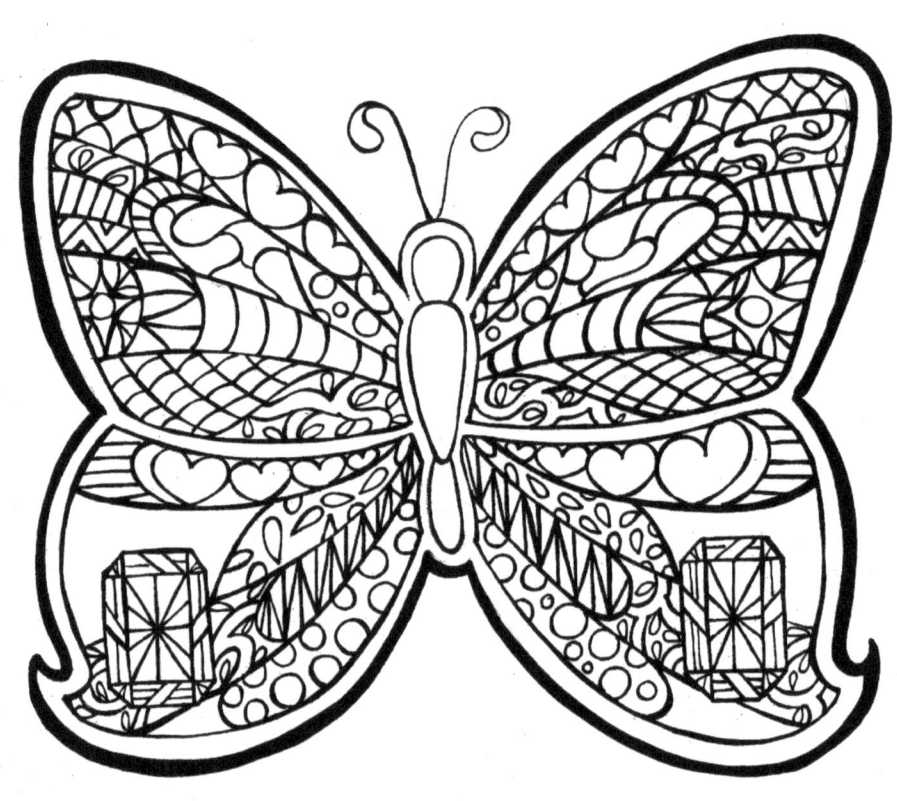

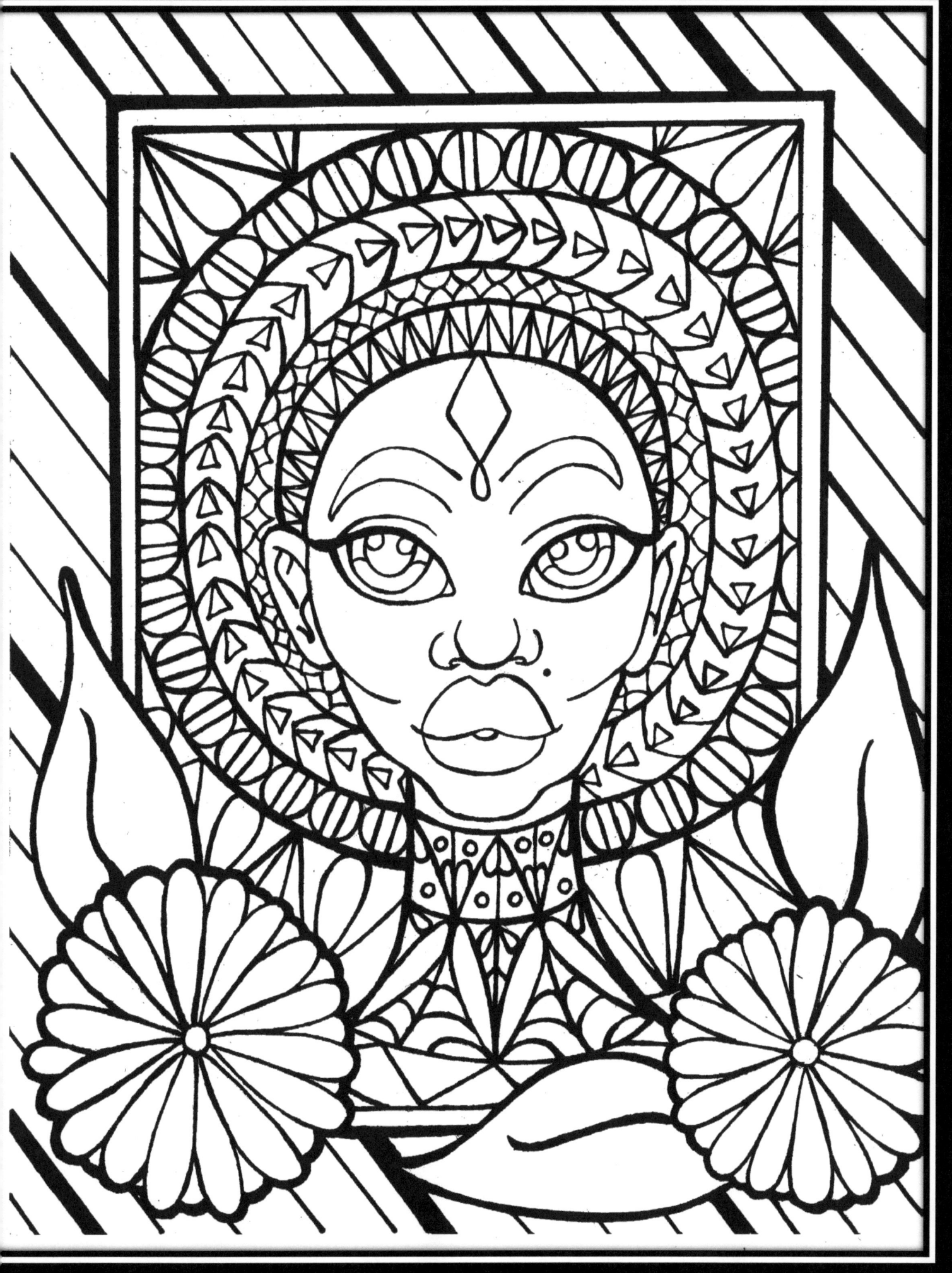

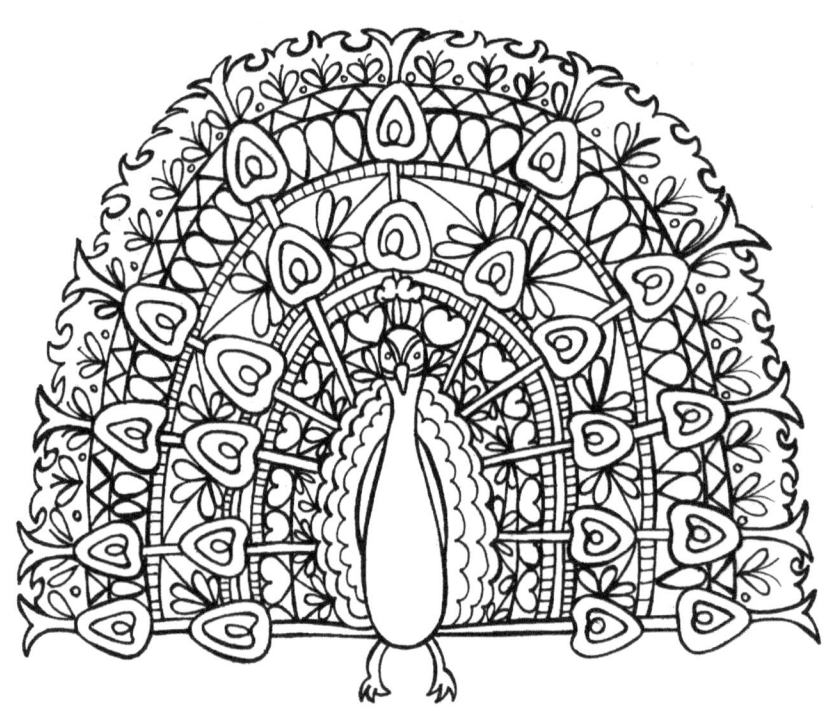

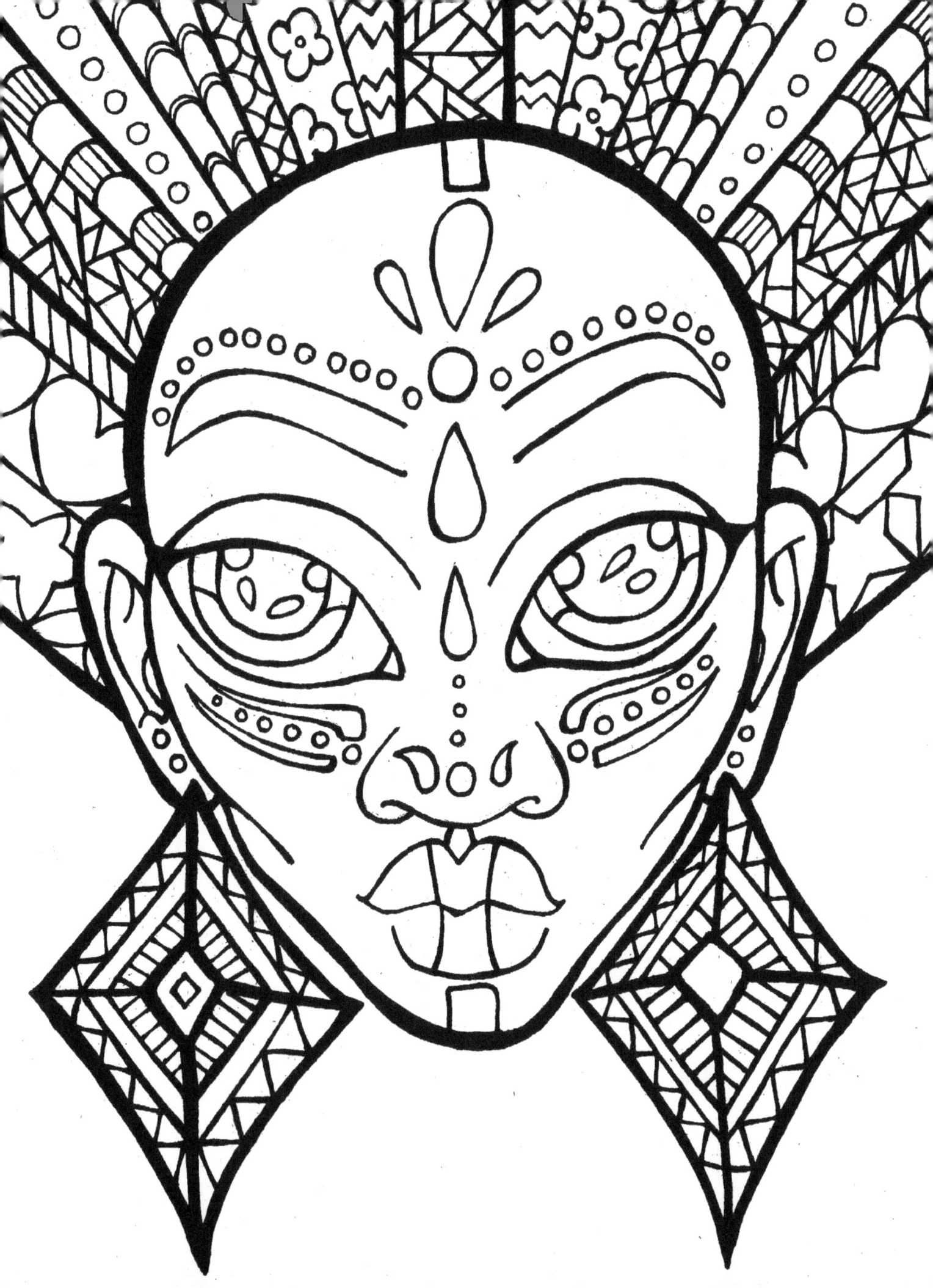

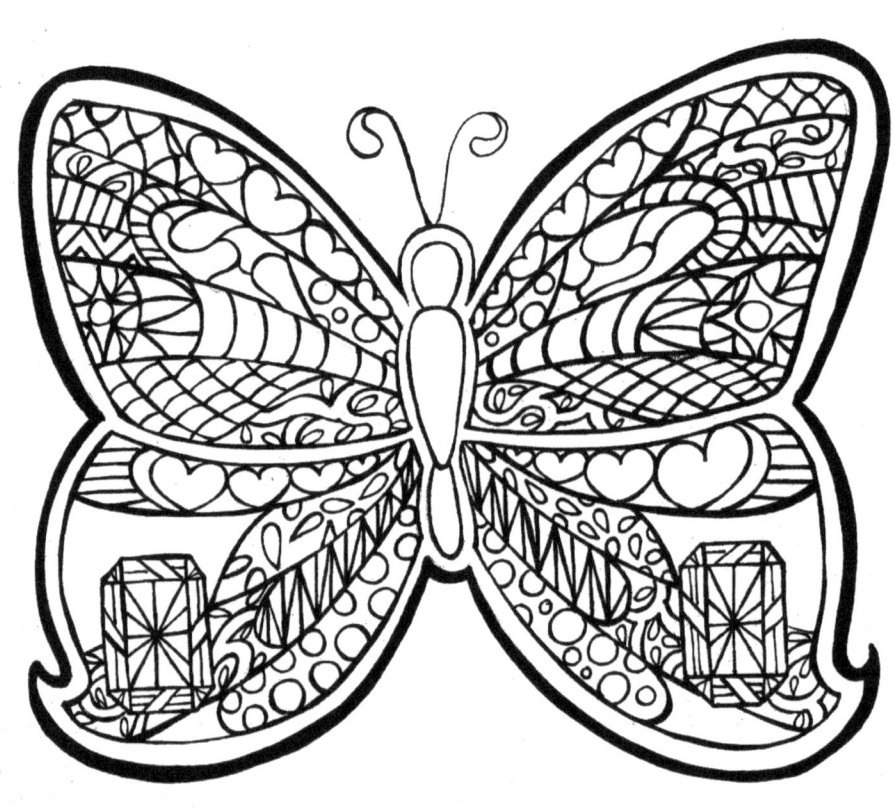

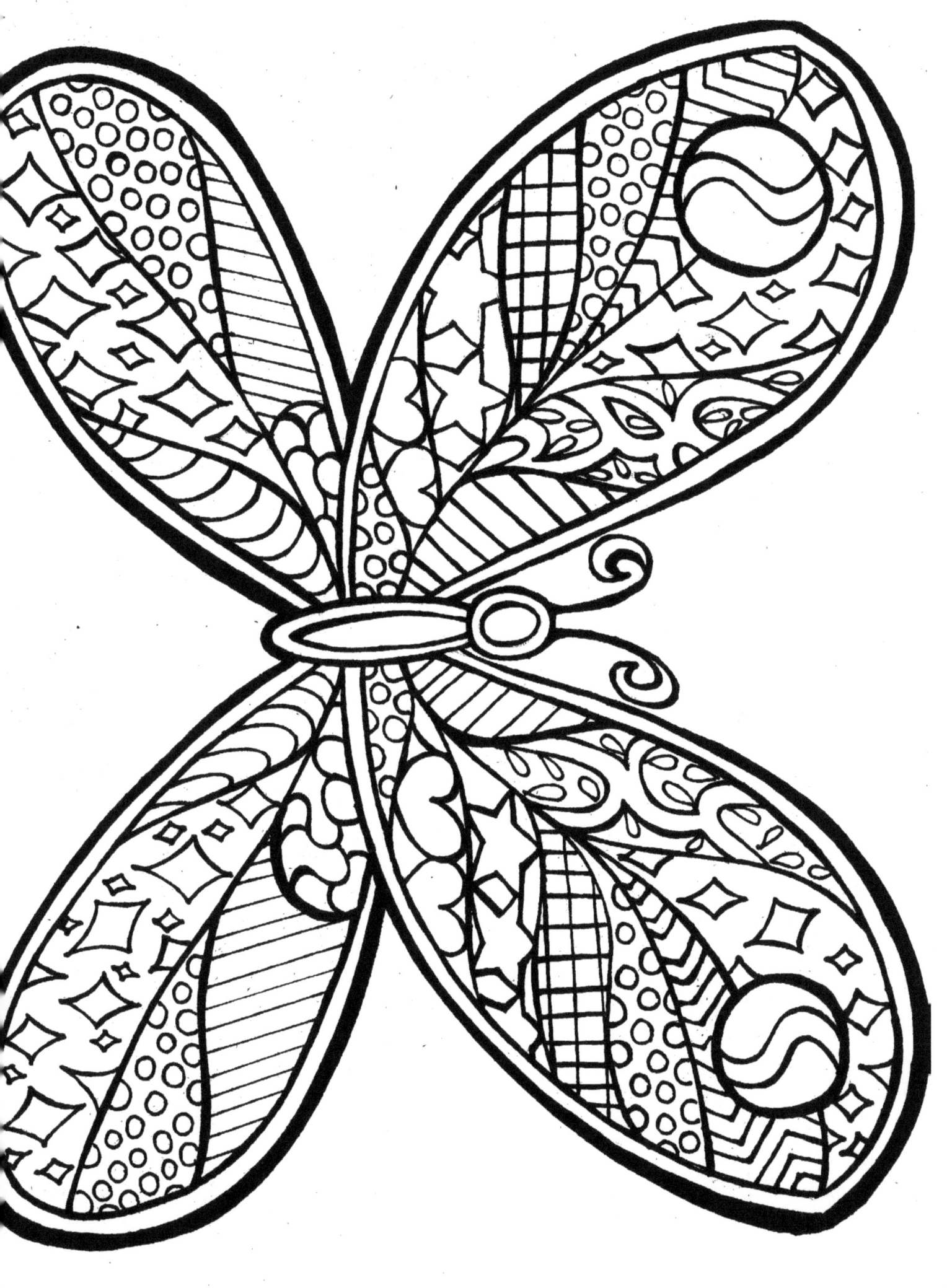

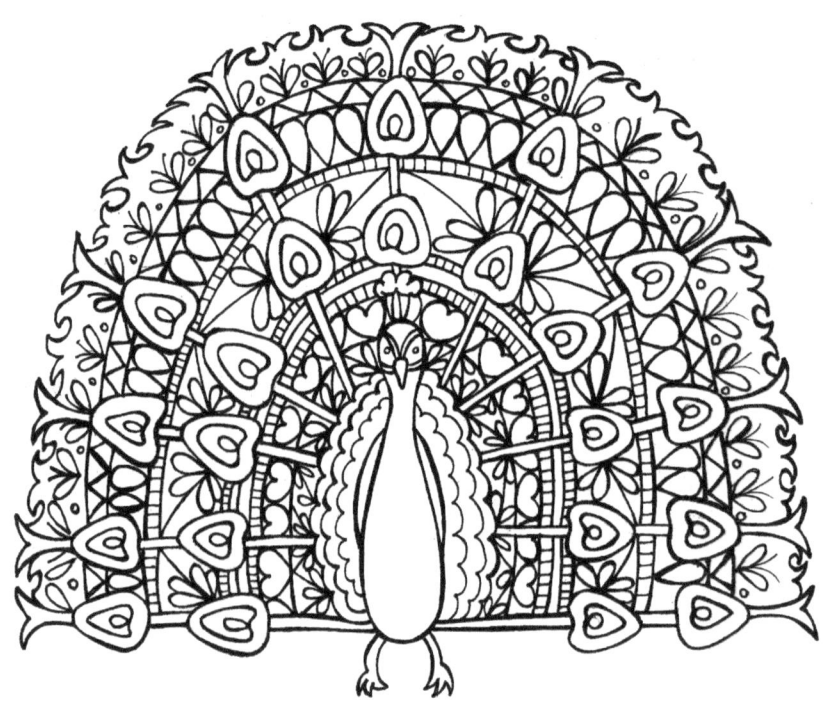

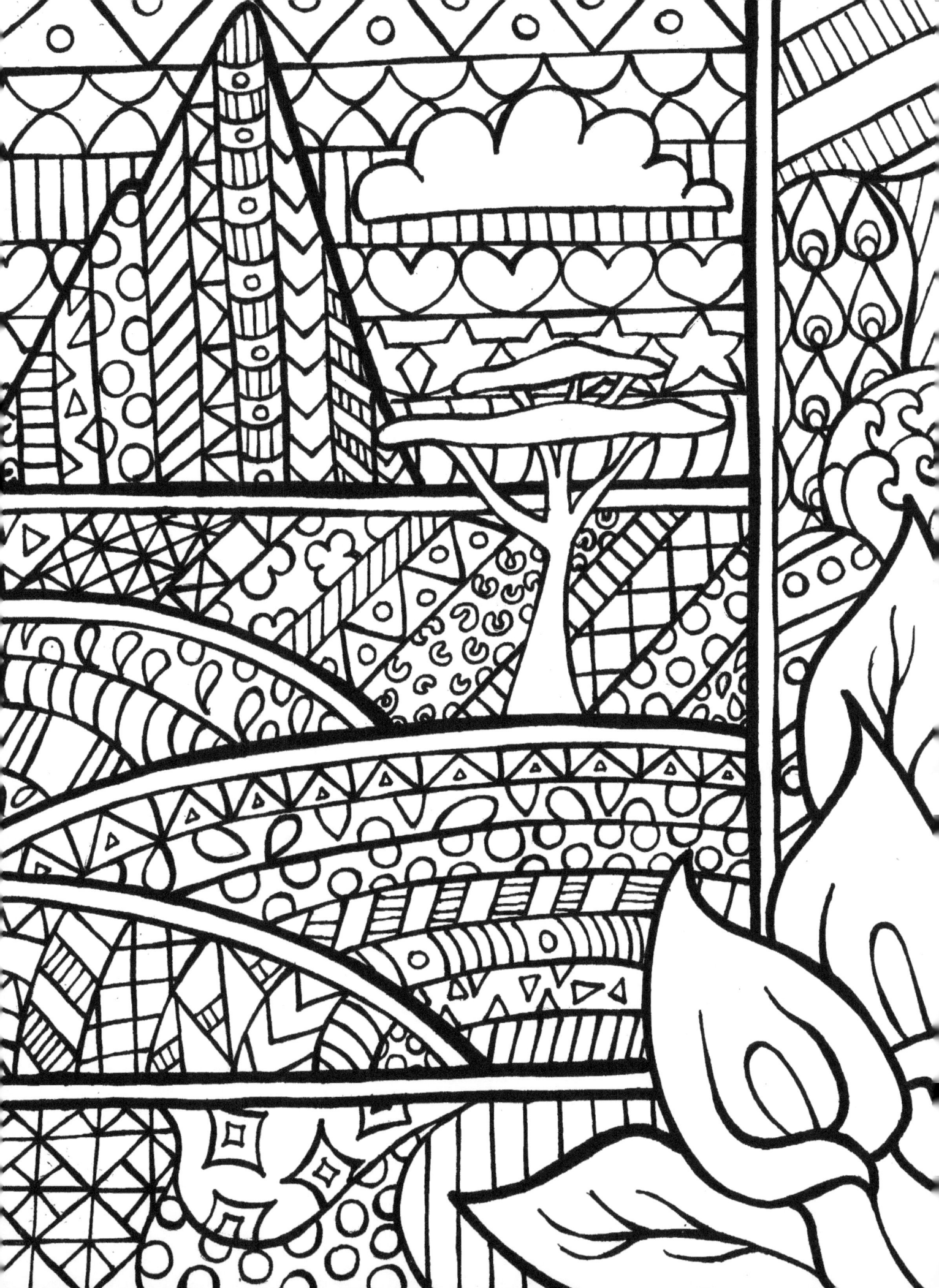

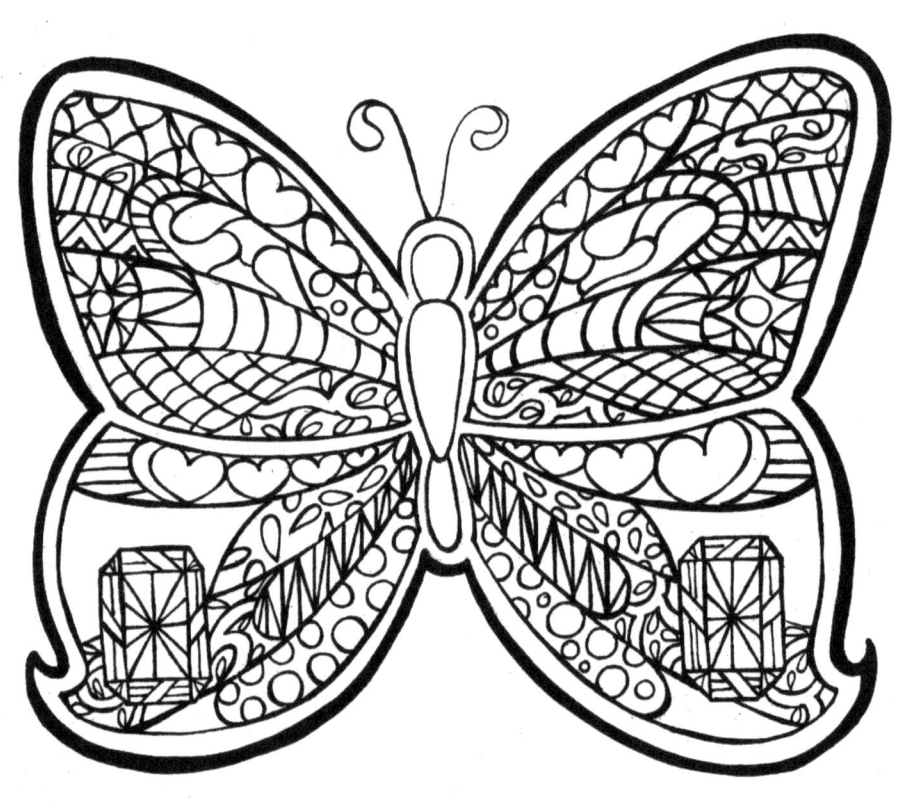

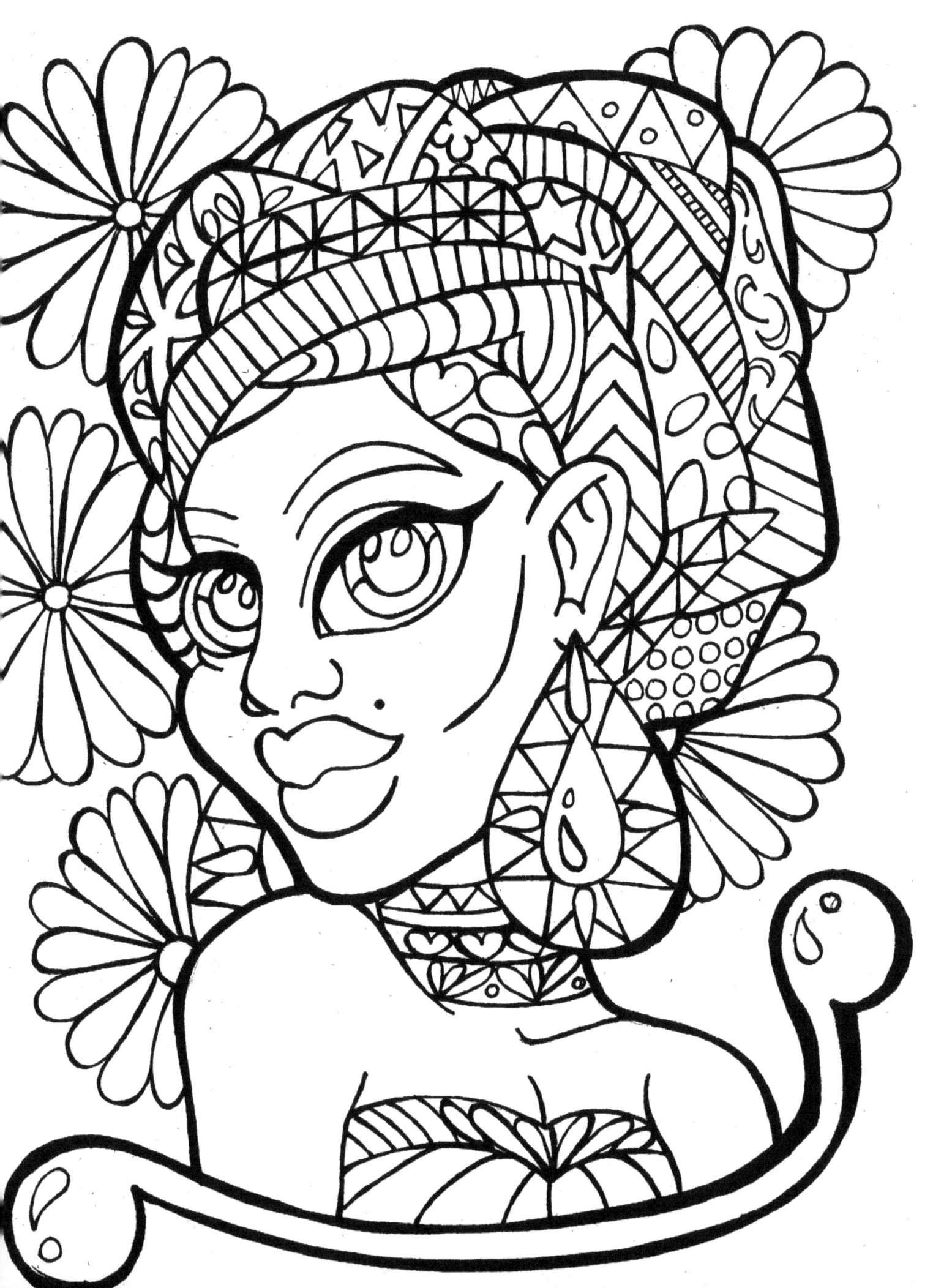

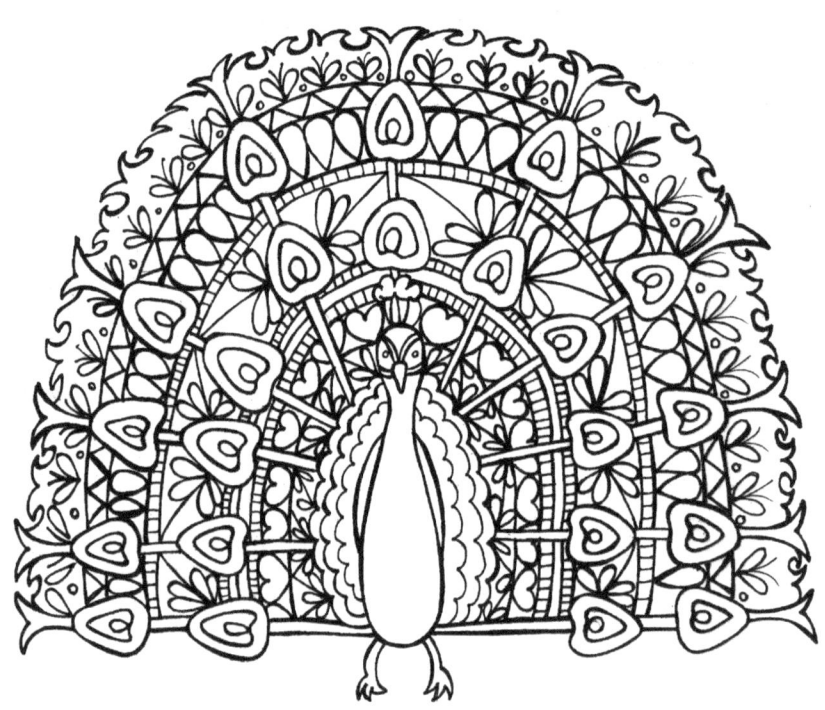

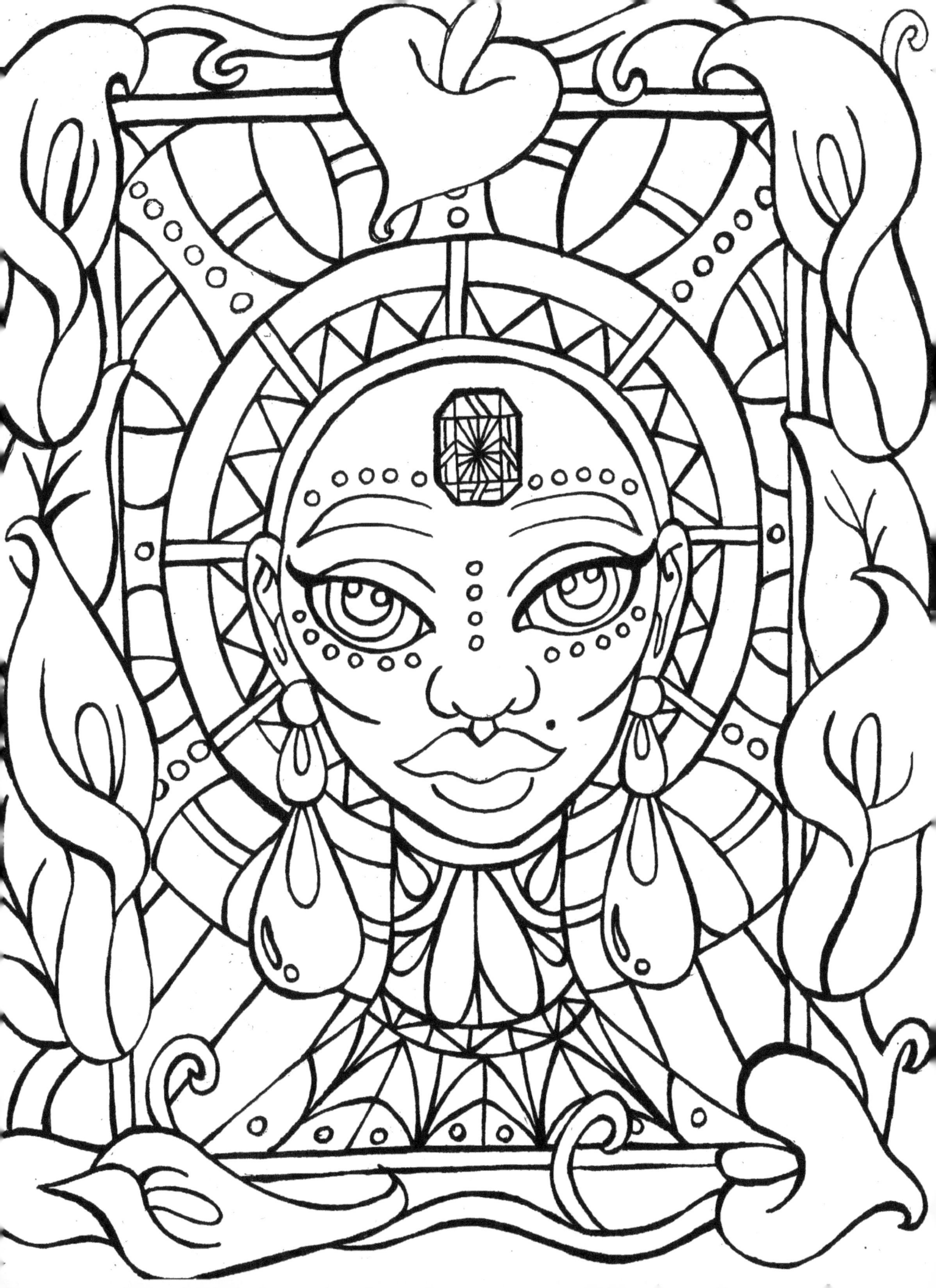

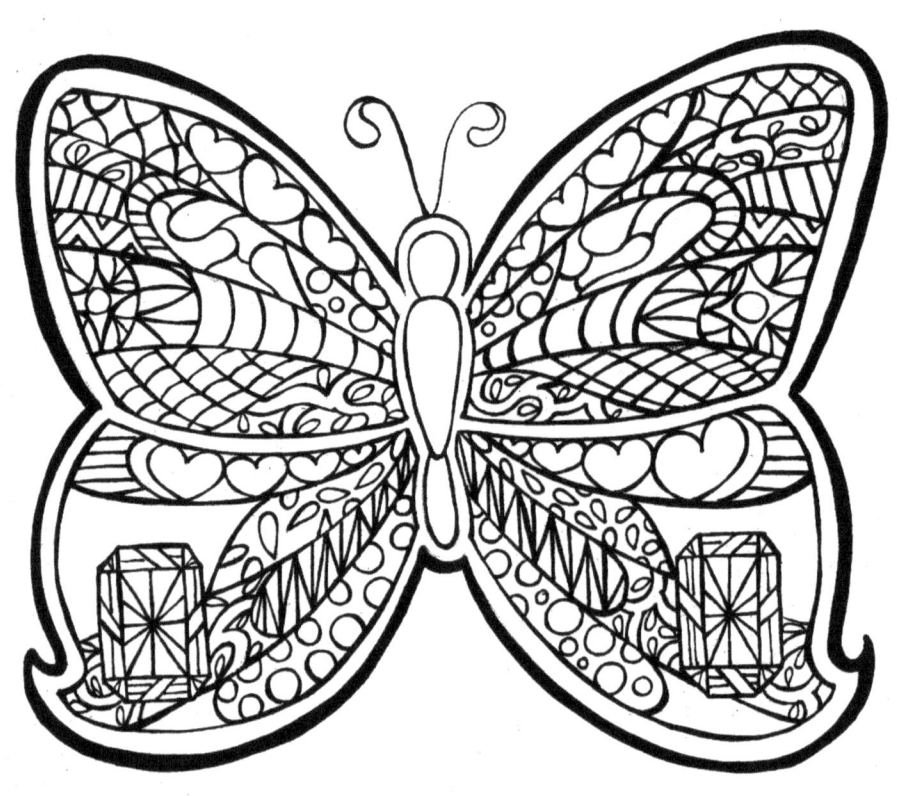

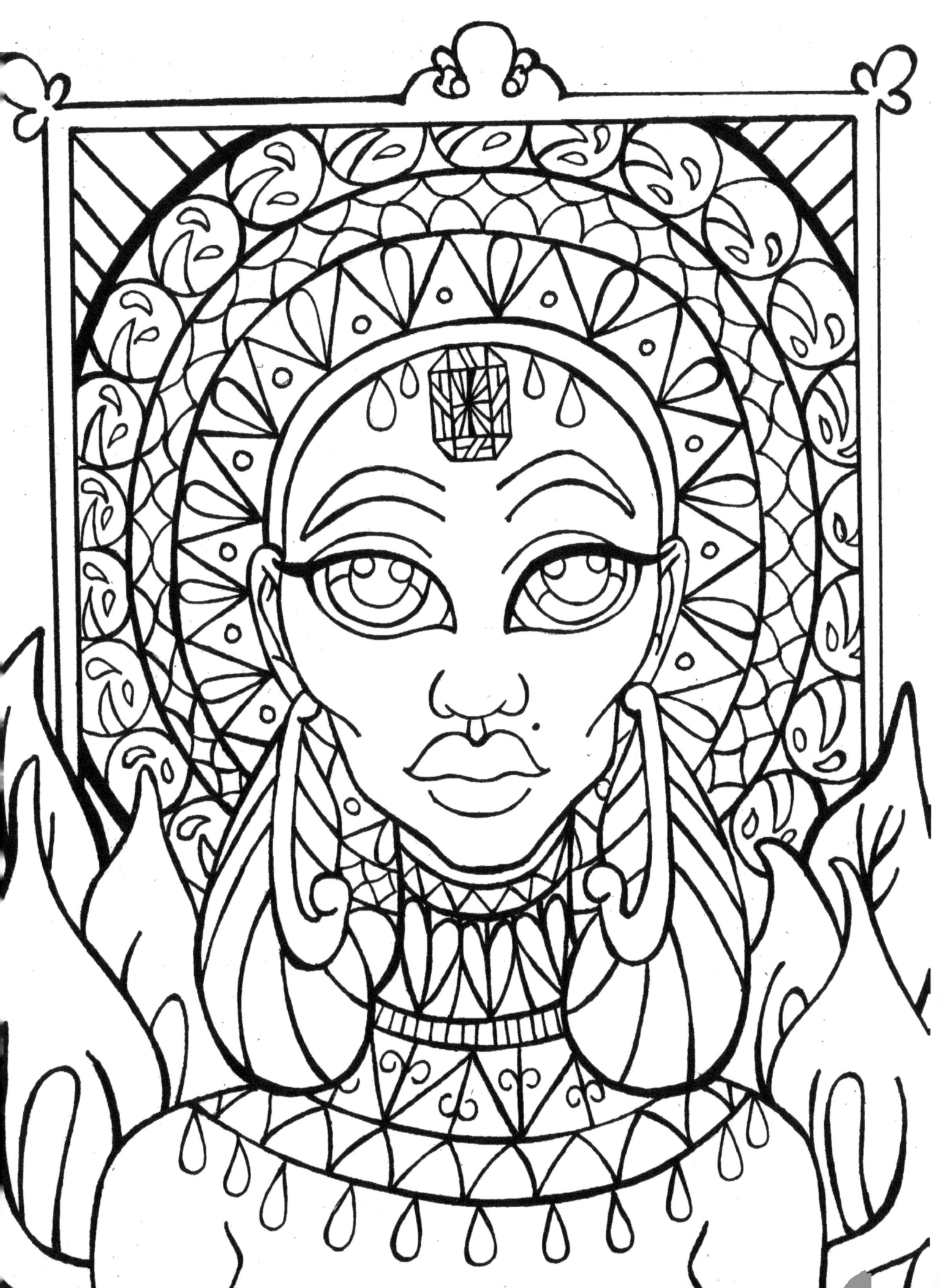

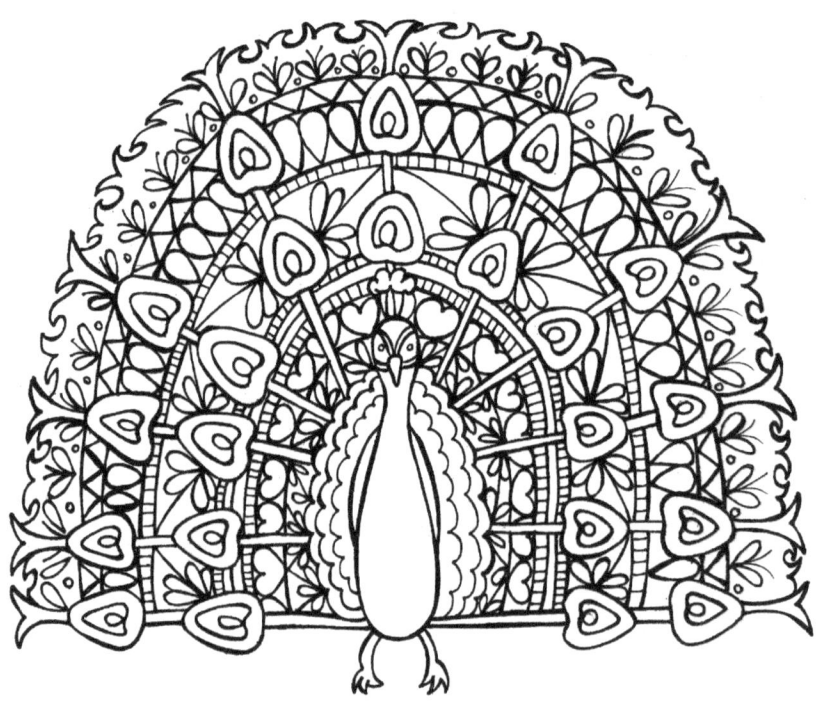

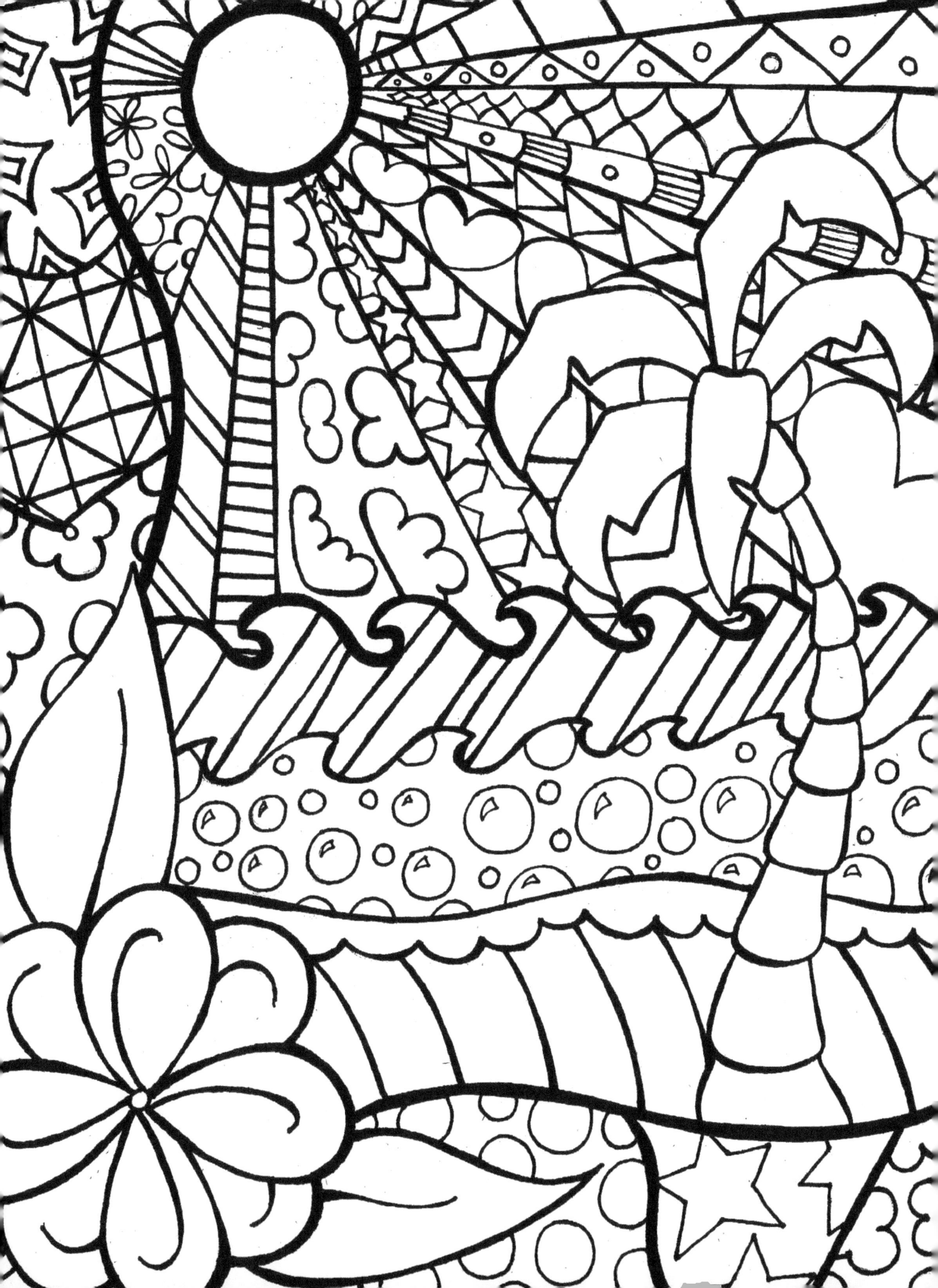

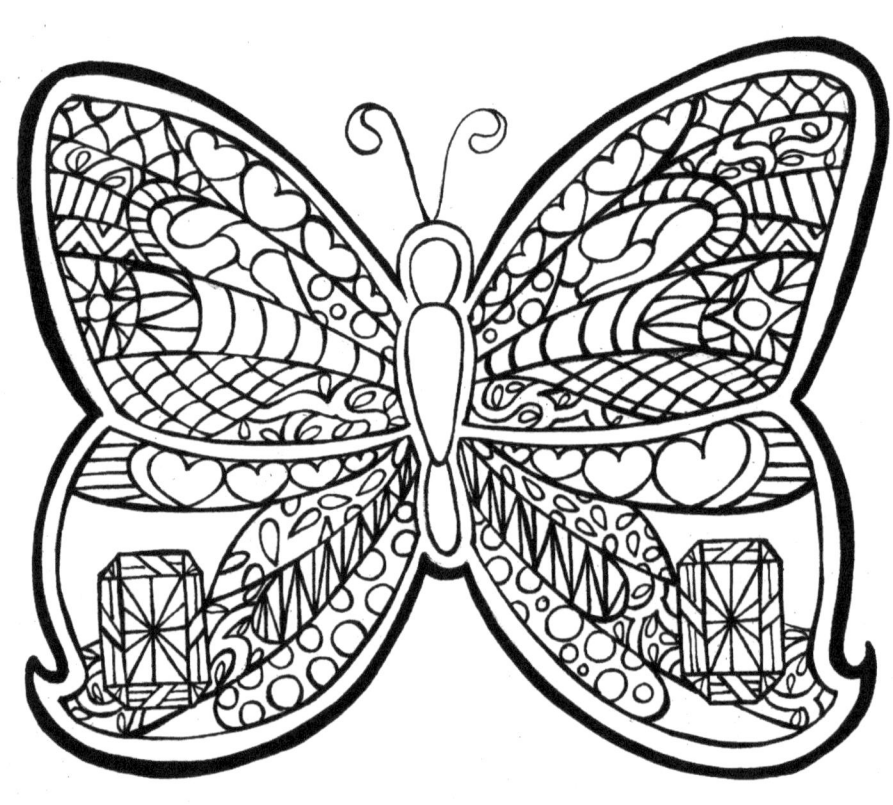

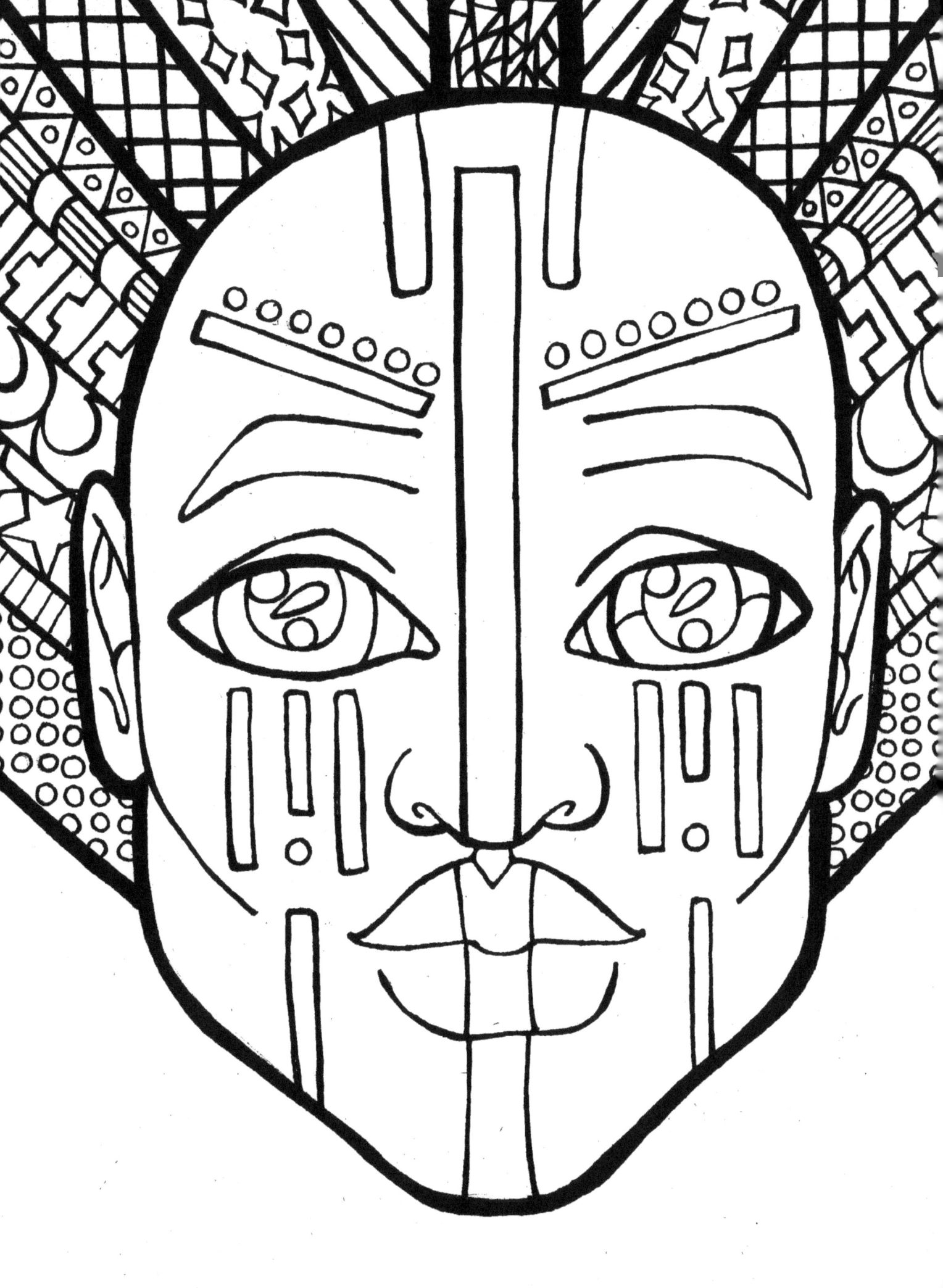

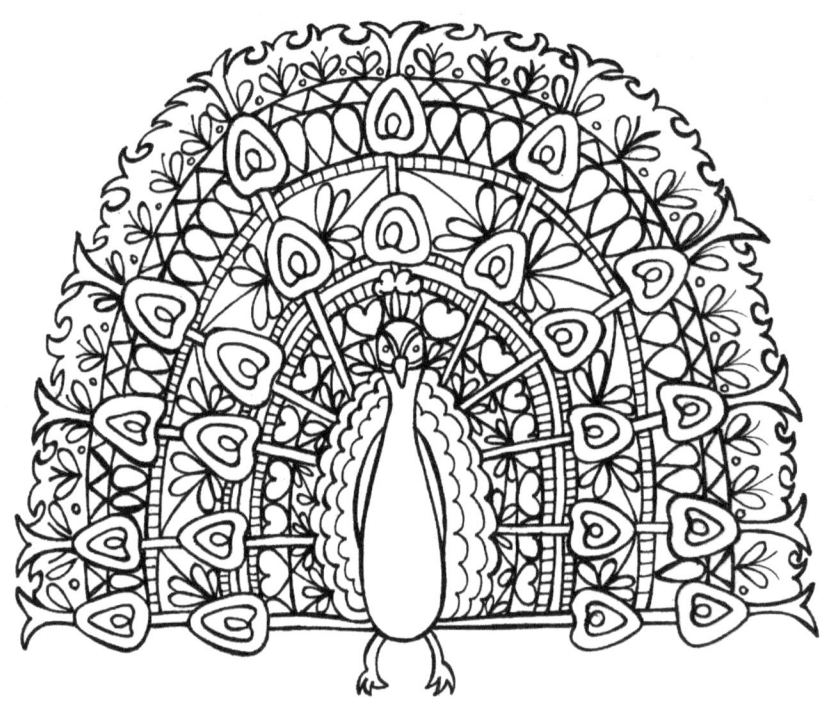

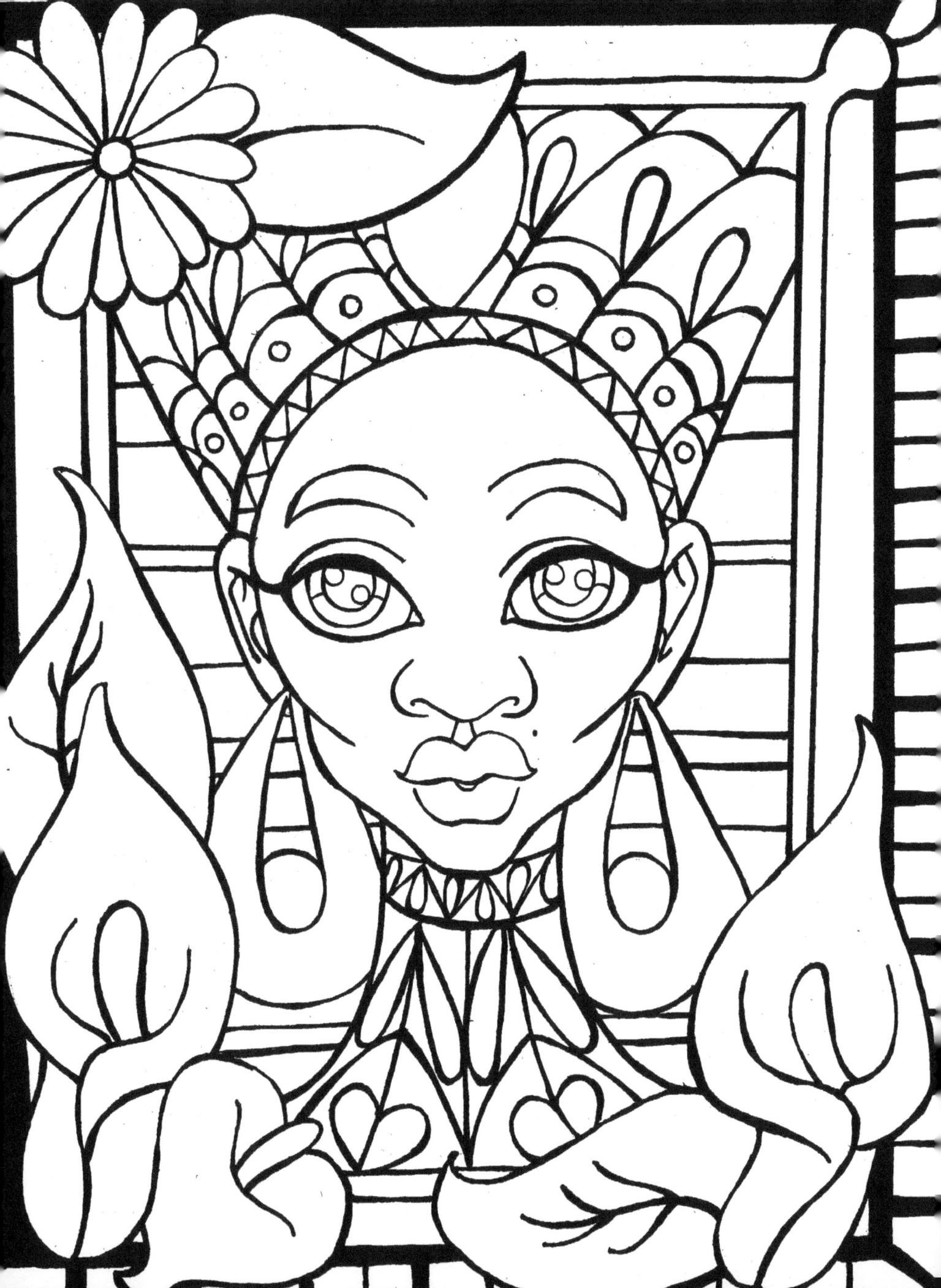

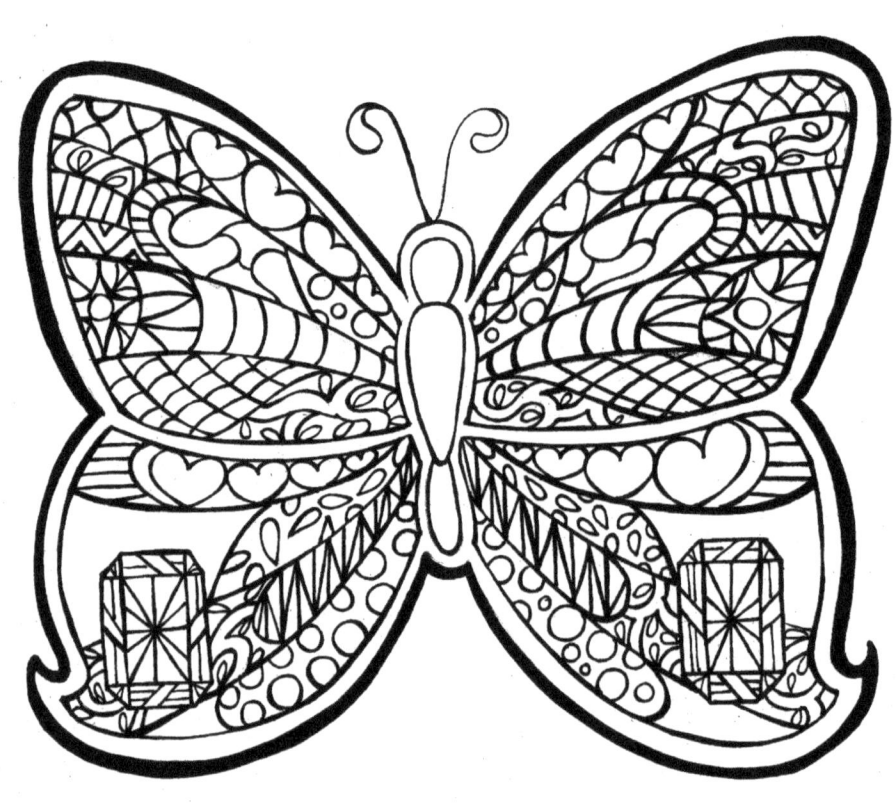

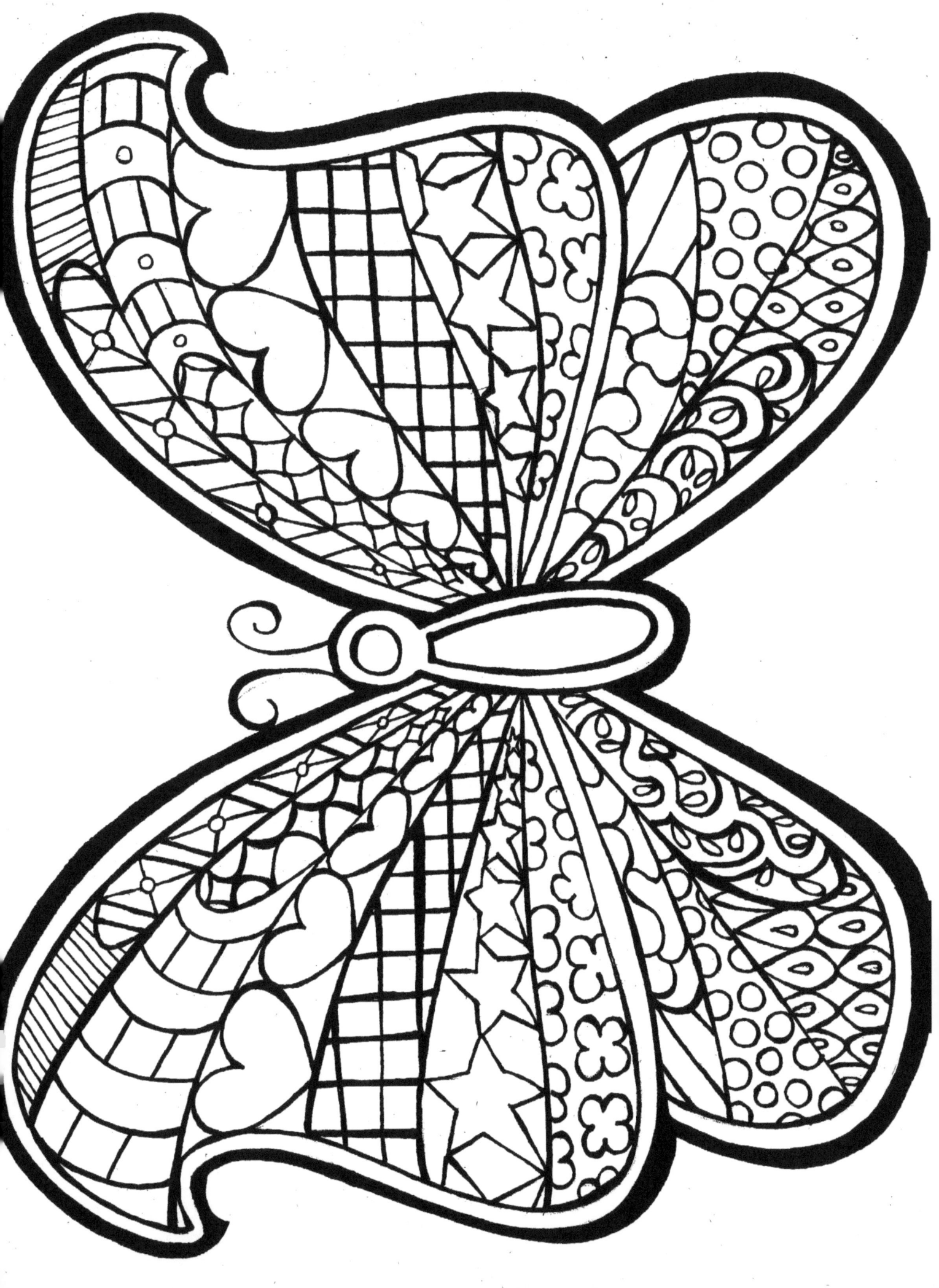

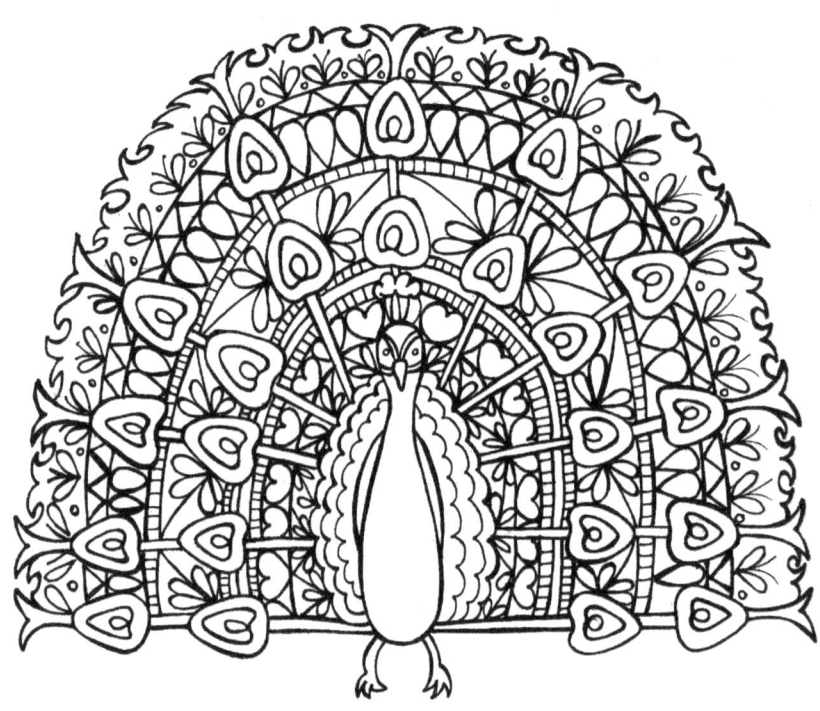

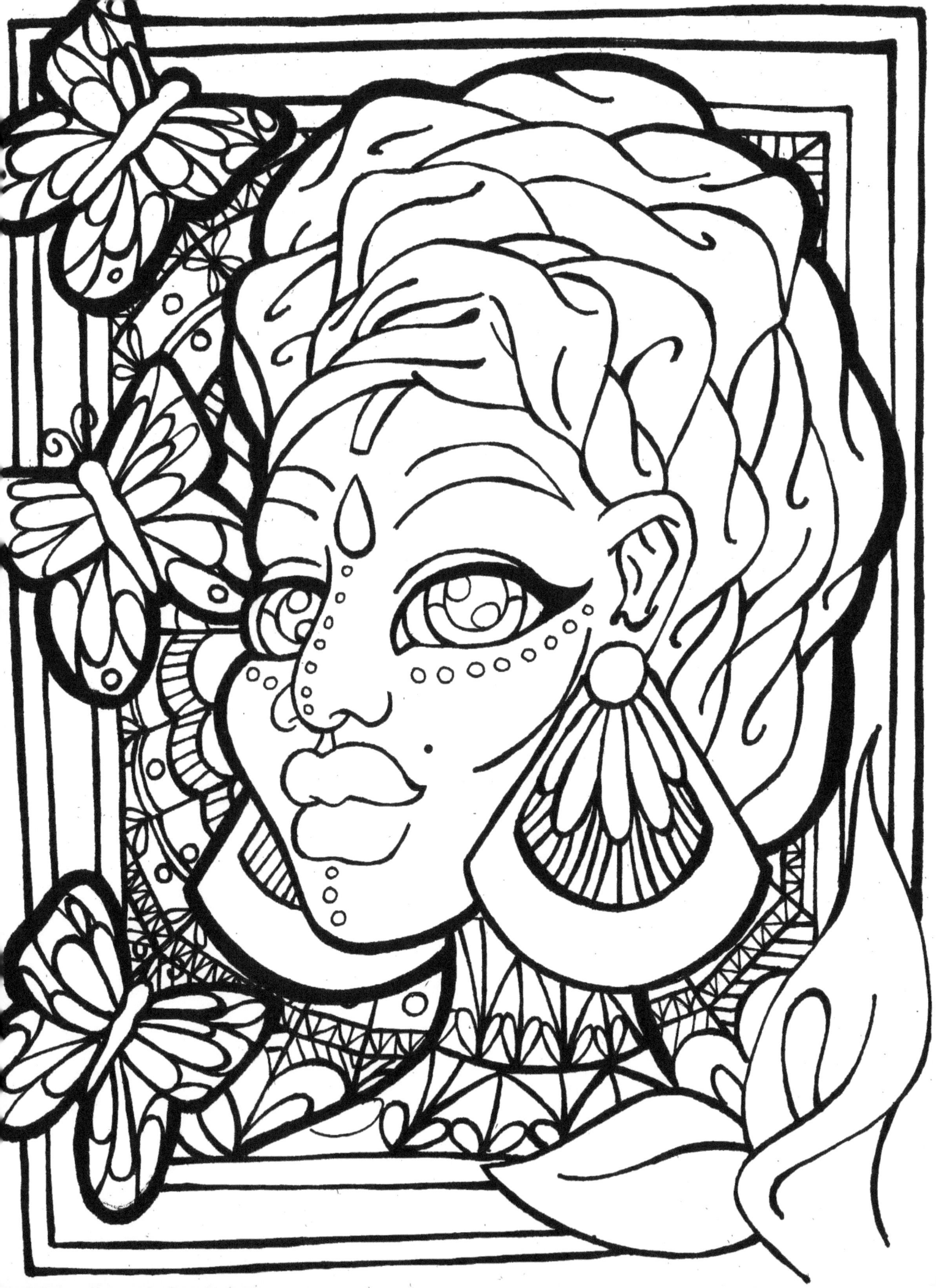

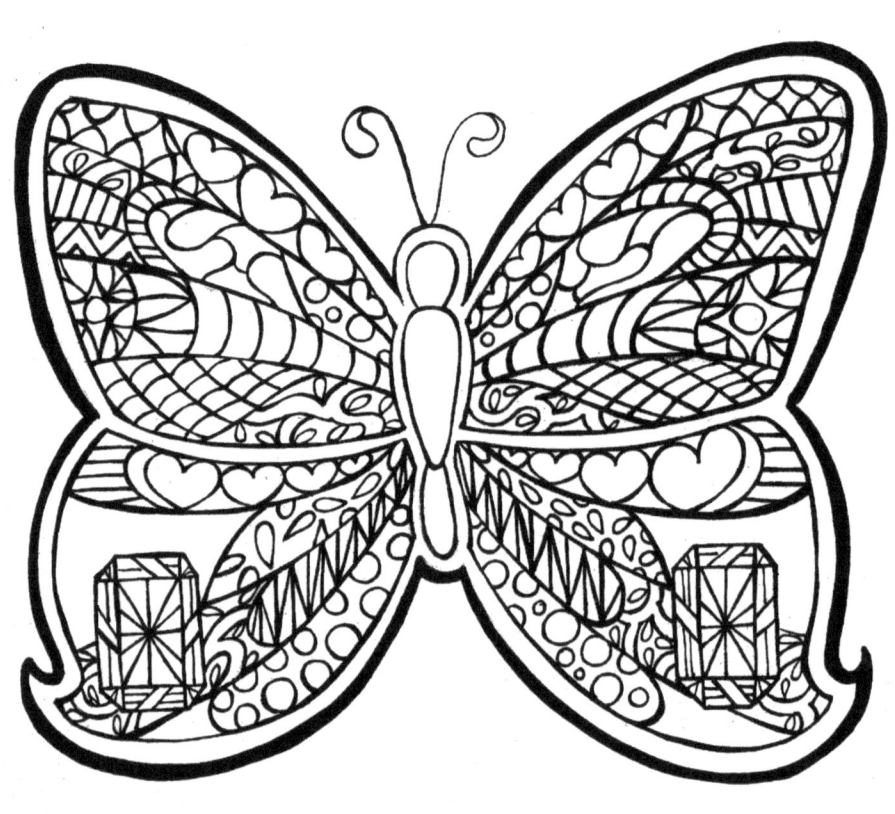

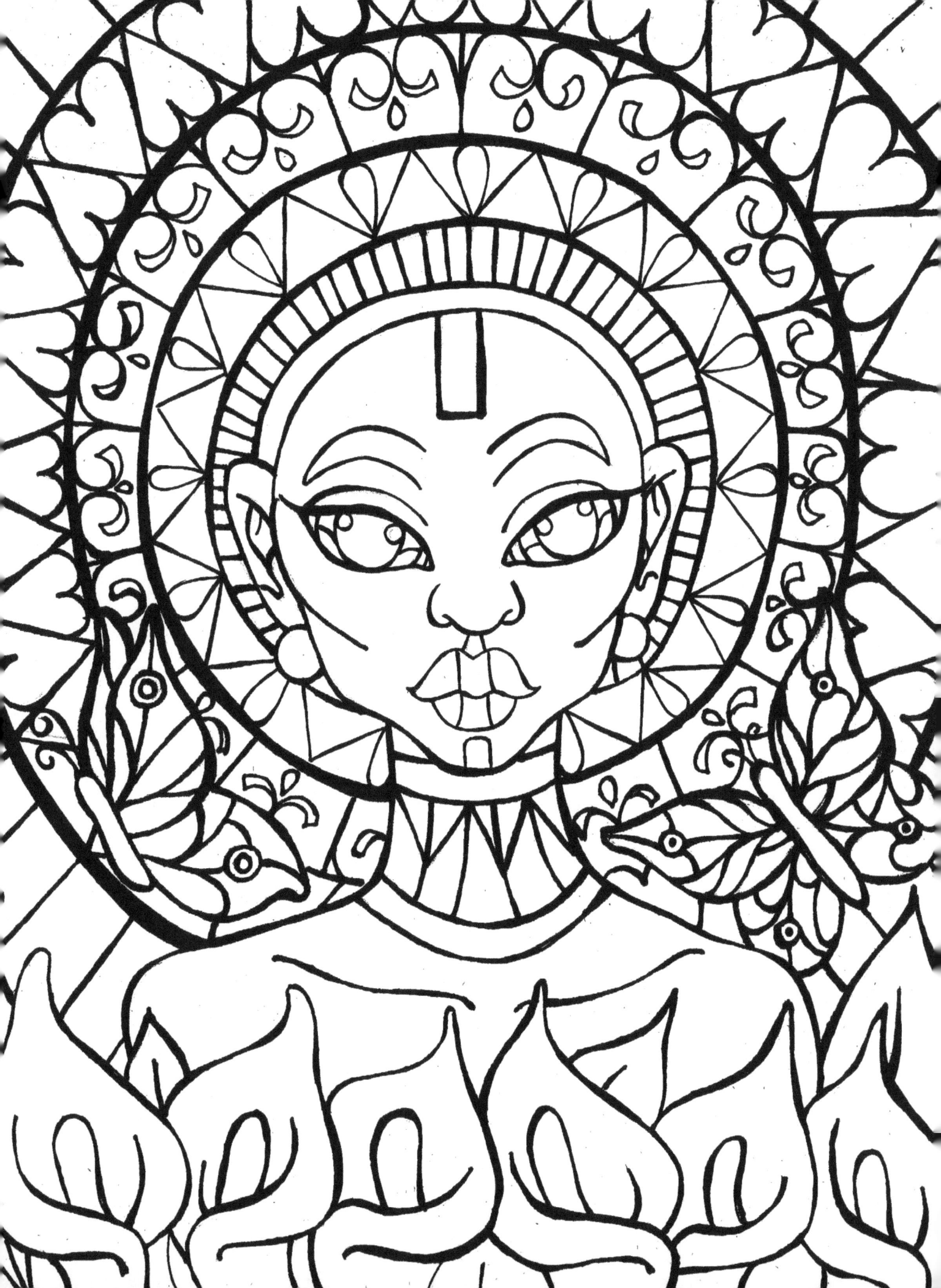

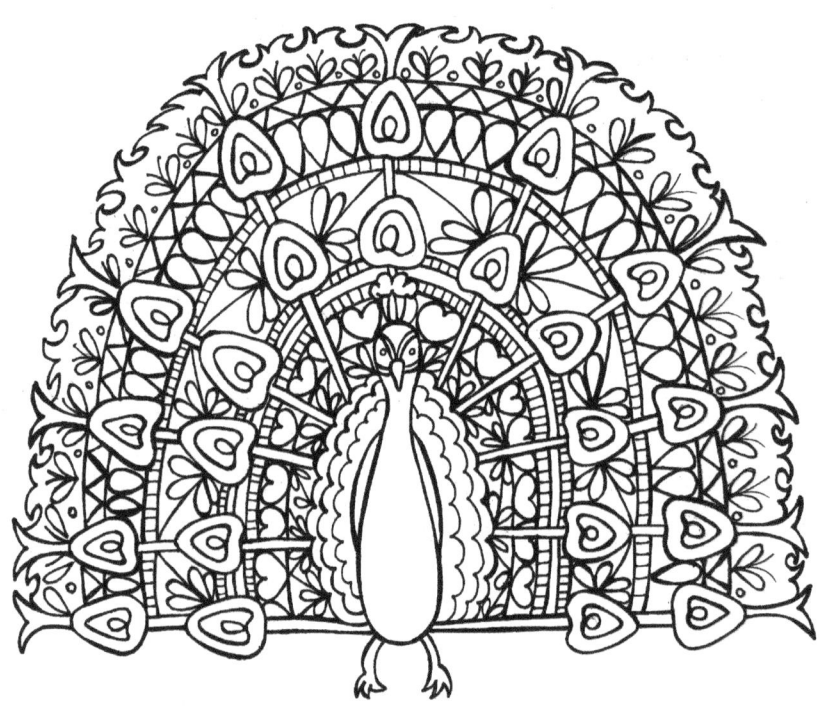

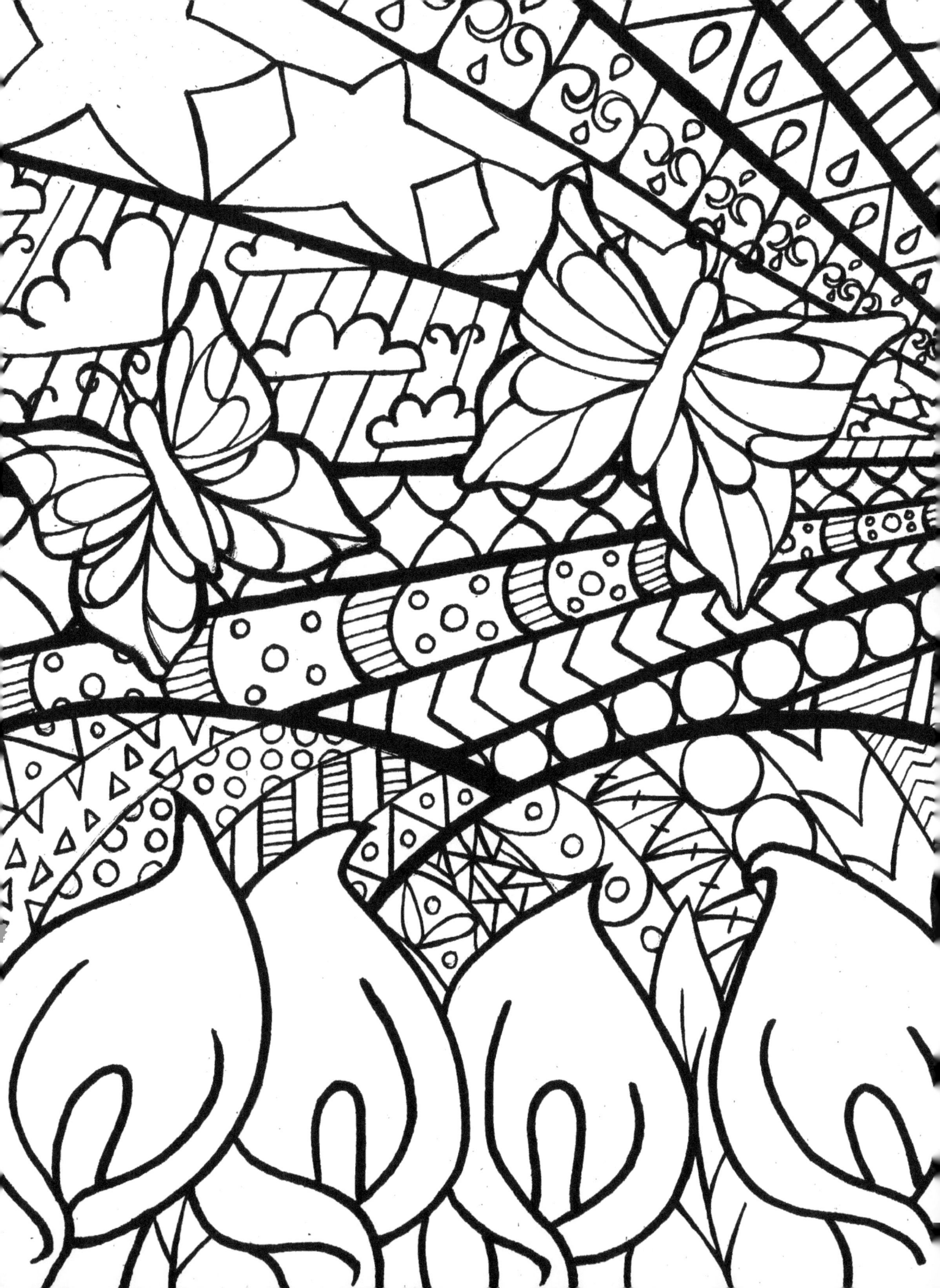

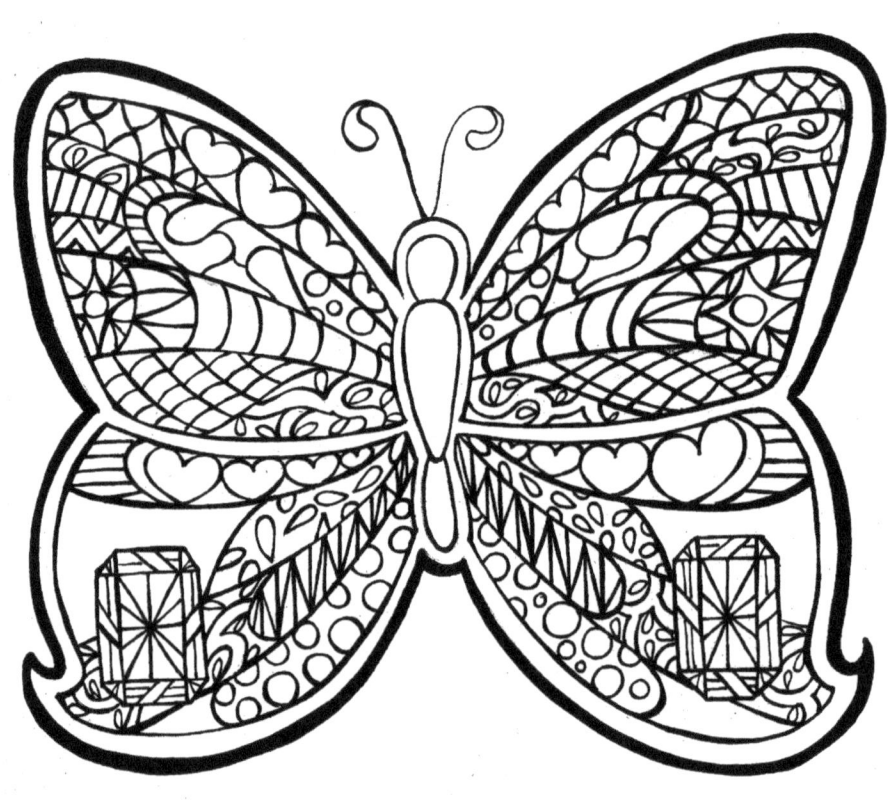

The Art of Akeem

Art Gallery

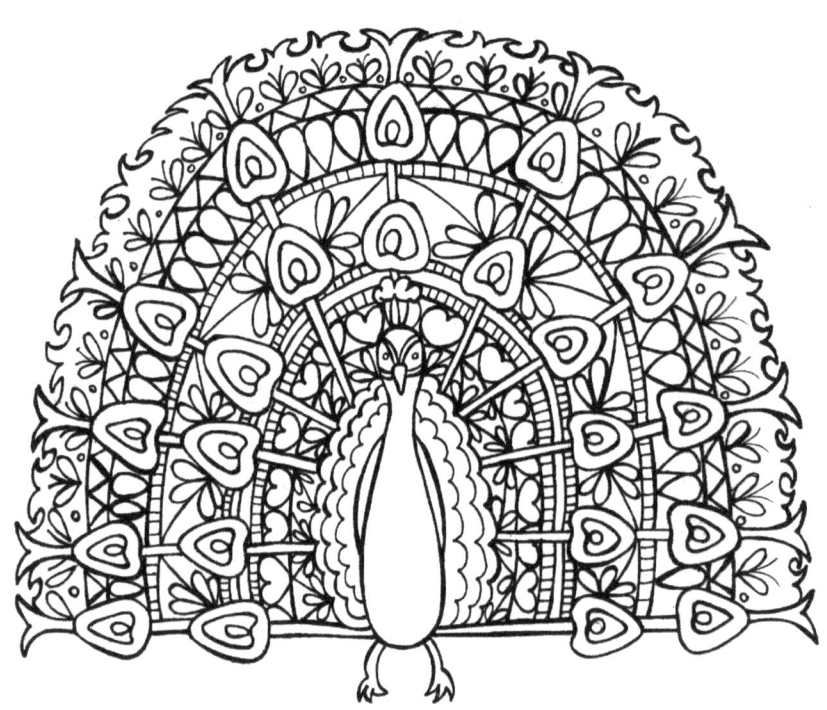

Illustrious Too features 26 hand-drawn Illustrations that allow you to become the COLORIST and Collaborate with artist Akeem Wayne to create some great Artwork inspired by Africa, Various African Cultures, and African People. As a thank you for your support of the arts, Illustrious Too features a Mini-Gallery of artworks by Akeem Wayne from his "Illustrious" Collection. Feel free to use the pictures of the artwork as a shading and color guide for your creations!!!

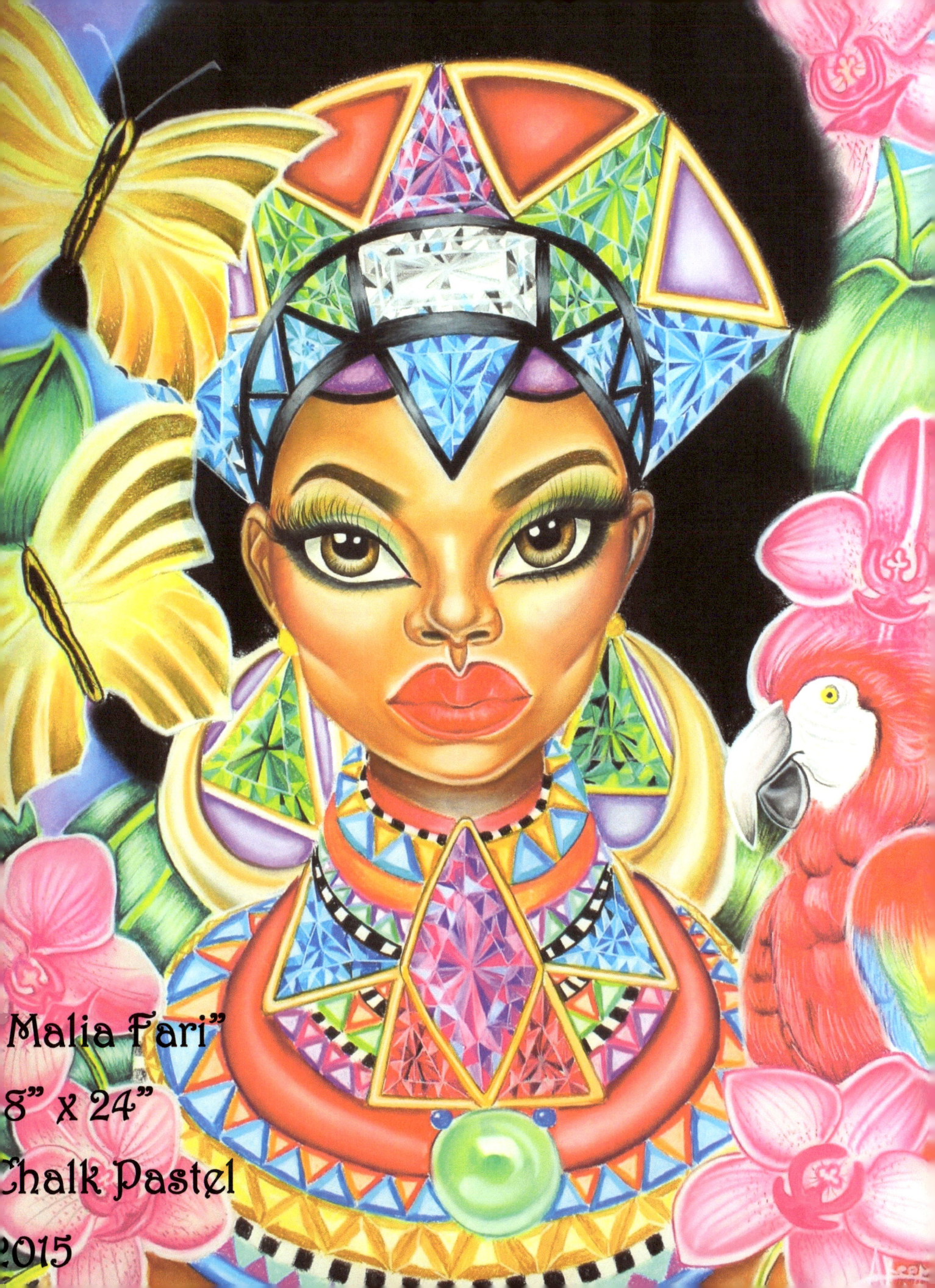

Malia Fari"

8" x 24"

Chalk Pastel

2015

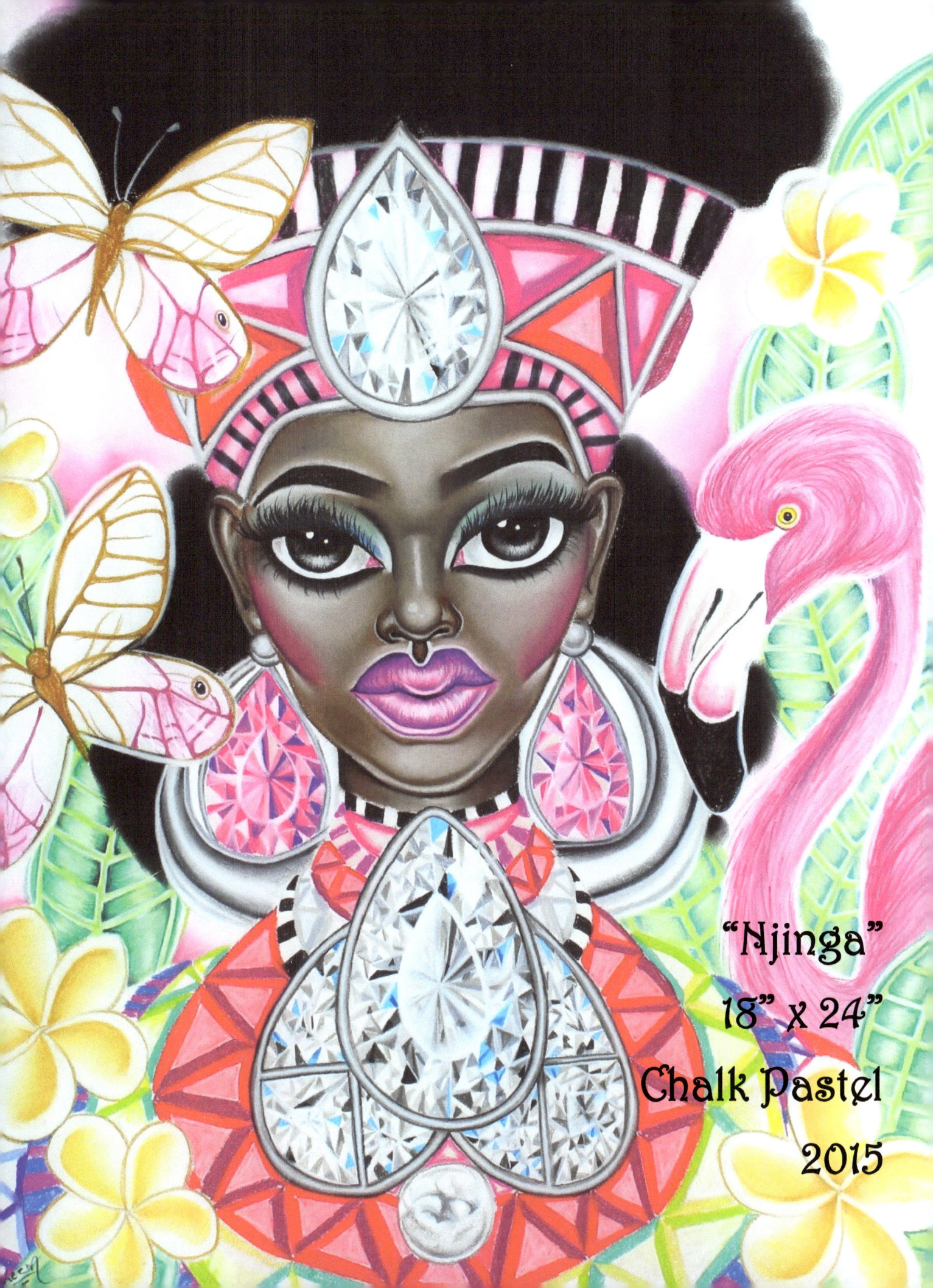

"Njinga"
18" x 24"
Chalk Pastel
2015

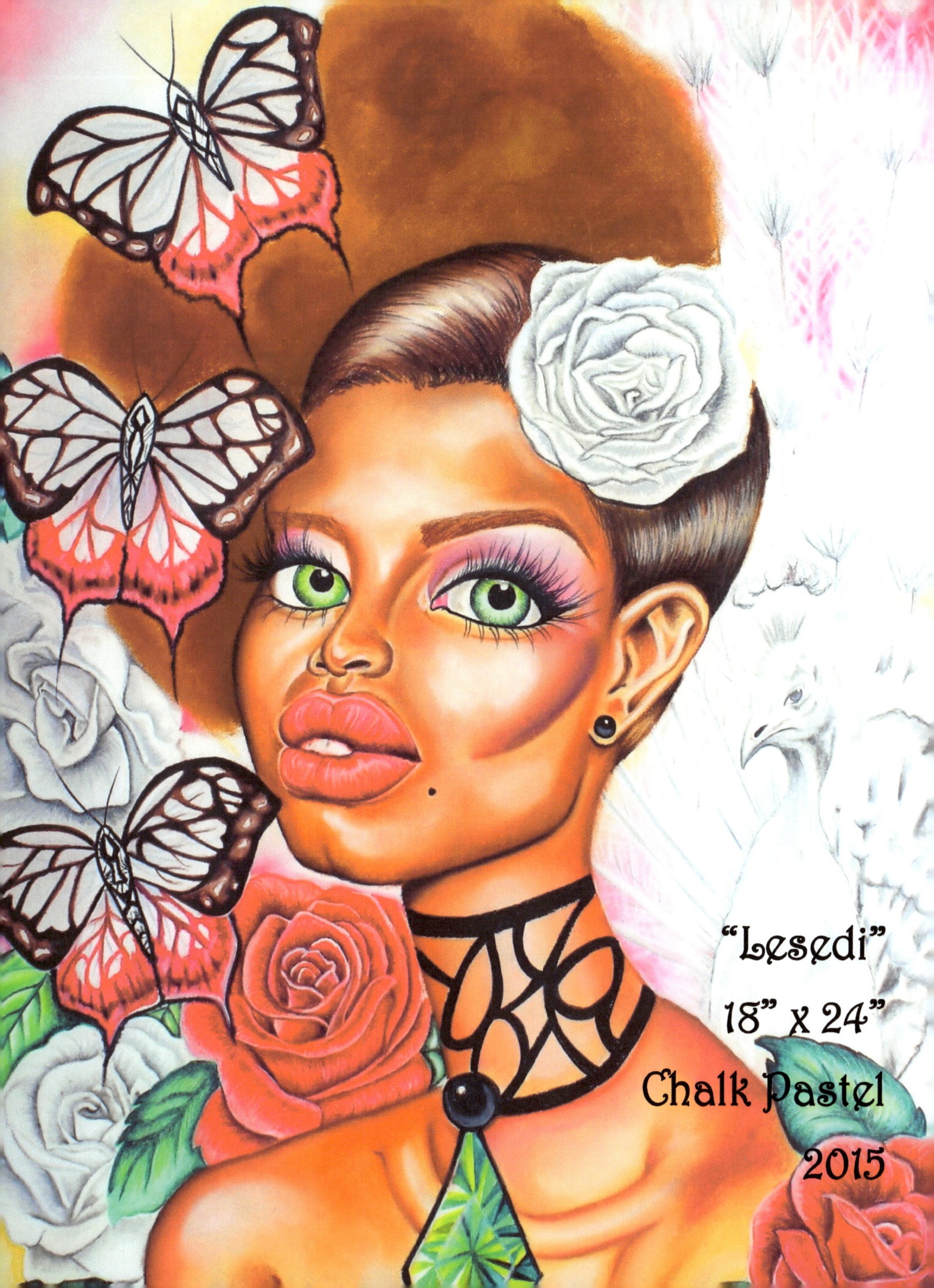

"Lesedi"
18" x 24"
Chalk Pastel
2015

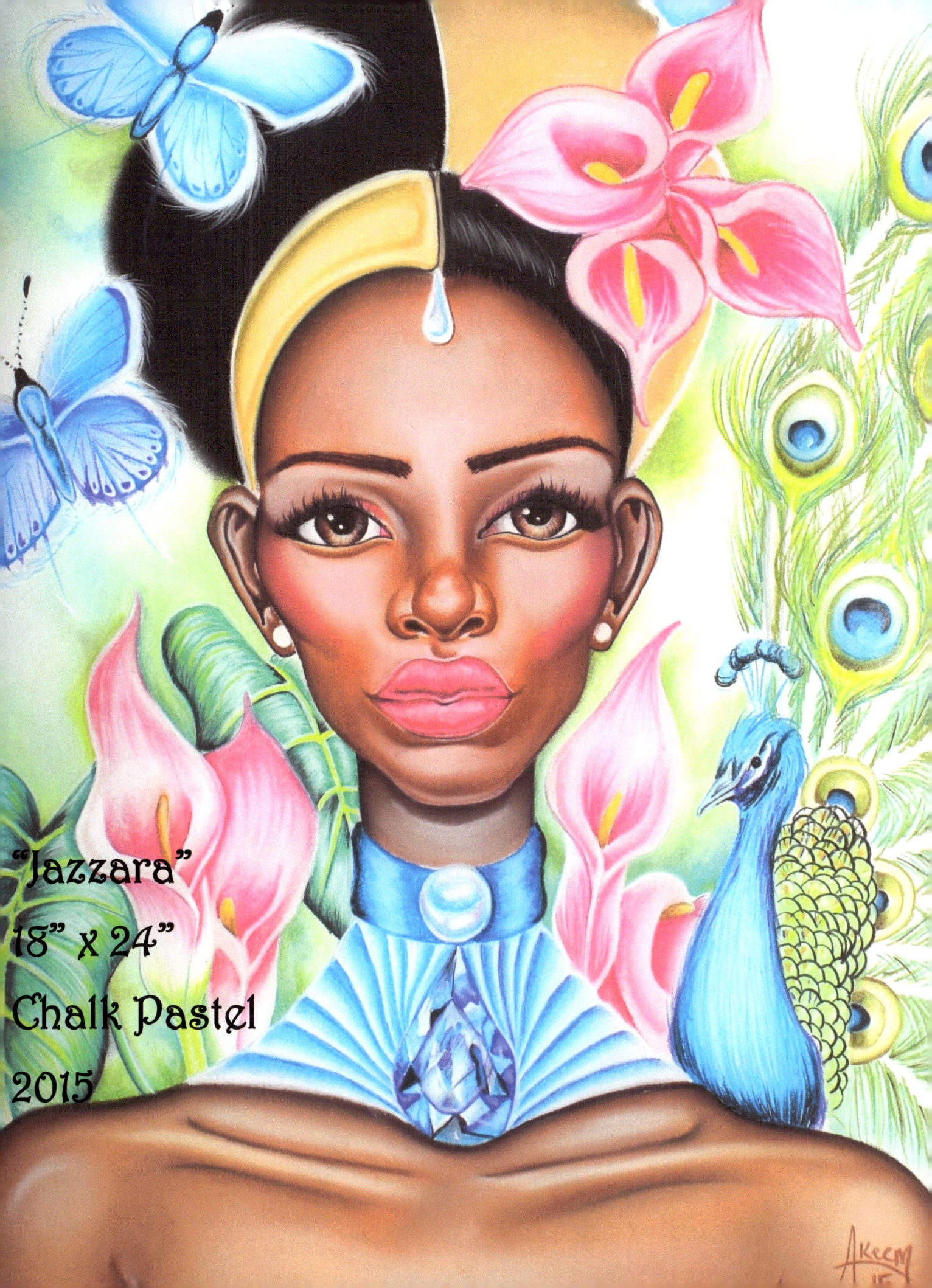

"Jazzara"
18" x 24"
Chalk Pastel
2015

Follow The Art of Akeem on
Social Media

IG: @TheArtofAkeem

FB: The Art of Akeem

www.akeemwayne.com

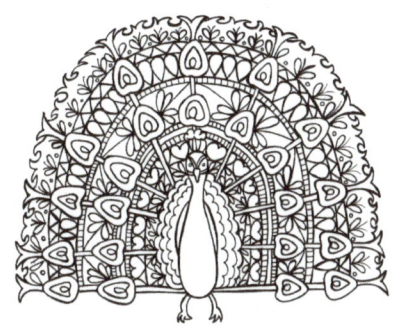